MW00627589

No More RESIDUE

17 BOLD, BRAVE, BEAUTIFUL WOMEN

Visionary – Crystal Cunningham

NO MORE RESIDUE

17 Bold, Brave, Beautiful Women

Copyright © 2020 by Crystal Cunningham

All rights reserved. No part of this publication may be reproduced, distributed, or transmitted in any form or by any means, including photocopying, recording, or other electronic or mechanical methods, without the prior written permission of the authors, except in brief quotations embodied in critical reviews and certain other noncommercial uses permitted by copyright law.

Printed in the United States of America

References:

Touch of God Ministries; Mori-West, Blogger, Dec 116, 2011 Stanley, Charles (2009) Life Principles Bible New American Standard Version The Holy Bible, TPT The Passion Translation

The Holy Bible, MSG The Message

Crystal Cunningham is an empowerment speaker, 2x Best-selling author, and The Extraordinary Woman-Life Coach. She is an unstoppable go-getter, dedicated to helping others become "Crystal Clear" in their life's purpose and vision. Relatable and down-to-earth, she has acquired, within the telecommunications industry, a 19-year tenure with one of the top Fortune 500 companies, Verizon Wireless. Her powerful message of hope, combined with her life experiences, empower and encourage people everywhere.

As the CEO of Crystal Clear Communications & Consulting, Crystal has influenced the lives of hundreds of women throughout her community. Through forums such as the yearly Women's Empowerment: Hats, Heels, & Lipstick and Crystallize Your Vision, she has facilitated a variety of open and honest discussions regarding various issues such as self-esteem, marriage, parenting, domestic violence, addiction, healthy living, and finances.

During her youth, Crystal experienced many different trials and tribulations, including teen pregnancy, runaway, abuse, and addiction. Her personal experiences were instrumental in her development into a true woman of inspiration who now helps others gain courage, confidence, and clarity within their own lives. Her first book, "Rise Up In Hope," encourages readers to live in their power and freedom to have a "Crystal Clear" life. She teaches the importance of owning your journey and ridding yourself of excuses or blame that hold you back. She highlights ways to overcome life's challenges and obstacles through faith, hope, and perseverance.

In her new and revised book, "No More Residue," which is a compilation of the stories of 17 women, Crystal is empowering women to rid themselves of their past decisions or experiences that secretly tormented them and kept them from moving forward. Crystal found herself in that same predicament after she relocated with her family to North Carolina. Being in that new environment shined a light on the shame that was hiding in the background. No matter what she did, she could not shake it. When it was time for her to embrace new opportunities that would elevate her in her career or relationships, the shame would show up. This persistent self-sabotaging of her life caused her to live in fear. If she was going to live a life of freedom, she knew that she would have to shift her mindset and embrace the process of truly becoming free. It was the secret of her addiction, failed marriage, custody battle of her son, and being a high school dropout that the enemy would use to torment her and caused her to struggle with her self-worth. Her belief system was affected and in need of restoration. Crystal did the necessary work that enabled her to be elevated to a new level of thinking and behaving. After writing Rise Up In Hope for the second time, she realized there was no more residue.

Although spearheading an anthology was not on her agenda for 2020, Crystal, inspired by the Holy Spirit, accepted the assignment without hesitation when God placed it in her lap and produced "No More Residue."

The stories are real and raw, and talk about EVERYTHING!

Contents

INTRODUCTION

Imagine you and me sitting together at a coffee shop or taking a long walk in the park just to breathe. Imagine every breath that you take becoming more alarming because there is something you need to say but can't find the words to say it. Let me ask you a few questions and see if you can relate.

Have you ever felt that you are all alone in your inner struggle hoping that no one finds out, but you can't seem to forget?

Do you constantly tell yourself that "you're okay" because that is what you want others to believe? Perhaps you believe that there's nothing that anyone can do, so you just keep it to yourself.

Are you carrying a heavy burden alone because you don't want to bother anyone else with your problem? Do you have the mindset that "you'll figure it out?"

Do you work non-stop and keep busy because the moment you slow down, you are alone with yourself and the quietness of your thoughts close in on you with condemnation?

Have you ever just wanted to "come clean" about something in your past that keeps showing up right before it's time to execute the vision?

Then this book, No More Residue: 17 Bold, Brave, Beautiful Women, is written for you. The purpose of this book is to encourage, empower and inspire other women to be confident, fearless, unashamed, and released from the fear of others knowing that their past decisions may have resulted in an unattractive lifestyle. These bold women shifted their mindsets, confronted their fears, disarmed their doubt and are now rocking their confidence and brilliance. Because they have provided real scenarios, lessons learned, advice, and resources to the reader, you will gain the strength and courage to once and for all say goodbye to the residue and embrace the brand new you.

Crystal Cunningham, Visionary –

Andrea Harley is an inspiring and motivational personal development coach, speaker and author. Through her transformation and connection to a higher power of her understanding, she has been able to overcome some of the darkest places in her life.

Andrea has experienced many trials and tribulations throughout her life including teen pregnancy, abortions, domestic violence, and drug addiction. These experiences have developed her into the humble true woman she is today. The woman that is dedicated to encouraging and helping others gain their courage, strength, and hope that they too can transform into a better person.

Through her story, "This is My Rock Bottom", she encourages readers to know that even at their lowest point in their life they too can turn their lives around. She highlights ways and steps to overcome life challenges and obstacles through faith, forgiveness and hope.

_____

Contact Andrea at: Website: andreajadeharley.com;
E-mail: andrea@andreajadeharley.com;
Facebook: Andrea Harley; Instagram: BelovedA70

This Is My Rock Bottom

Andrea Harley

M ay 4, 2008 was the day I surrendered, and my entire world changed. At the age of 38, I was a single mom of three. I was struggling with a disease of addiction to drugs for 14 years. The home that I shared with my children and my boyfriend was the hangout spot. If you came through, you knew we were going to have a good time. The traffic in and out of my house was crazy. You know, like the revolving doors we use to enter buildings? Yeah, that was my house. My children made it to school every day, I kept a roof over our heads and food on the table, so, to *me*, we were good. I considered myself a "Functional Addict," as some would say. That was until Child Protective Services (CPS) arrived at my doorstep.

In April 2008, CPS came to my home because of an anonymous call they received about me using drugs with my children in the house. That was a form of child abuse and neglect. Not me, the Functional Addict. I was in denial big time. I was given a drug test and I tested positive for cocaine and marijuana. It was mandated that I attend a 12-step drug program. Not by myself, I had to drag my kids there as well. I was so angry I wanted to draw blood. I was going after everybody in my family. I was ready to fight. Me being the vindictive person I was, stopped talking to everyone. My family wanted me to lose my kids, so we were dead to them. The program provided transportation to and from the program. The van came every day like clockwork to pick us up. I felt so humiliated and embarrassed. Not the fly girl from Harlem on a drug rehab bus! Nah, this could not be real.

I attended the program every day, and once I returned to my home, I would use again and again. That embarrassment I felt earlier that day went right out the window. Have you ever felt like, "I am grown, so I can do whatever I feel? I am functional, and my kids want for nothing." I had a live-in boyfriend waiting for me. We would use drugs as if it was another regular day. I had so much to lose, but I just would not stop using. I failed every drug test while in rehab. One day I went to my counselor begging and pleading to go in-patient.

I knew that my life and the life of my kids was on the line. On Friday, May 2, 2008, I decided not to go to the program. I had been hanging out, using drugs and partying the night before, so I was in no condition to go. I figured I had the perfect excuse because we were celebrating the upcoming birth of my first grandchild. On Saturday, May 3, 2008, CPS came back. They had received a call because I missed the program the day before. They could see we were getting ready to go out. They did their assessment and left, but this visit just did not feel right. I was upset and disappointed with myself. I was so distraught and just wanted to give up and not live anymore. I was confused and asked "why me?" A good friend talked me into going to the baby shower. He even escorted me to and from the venue. After the party, I returned home and made that call once again. I cried and cried all night to my friend while using. I realized I not only was I killing myself; I was jeopardizing losing my family. I was sick and tired of being sick and tired. That night I decided that enough was enough. I had to do something different to get a different result. That night was the last call I ever made for drugs.

That Monday, my CPS worker came to my home to remove my kids. I argued and fought with them to get out of my house. I begged them to give me some time to have someone come and get them to keep them from going into the system. I knew if they went into the foster care system, I would have lost them forever. My son's father managed to get there in time to get my two youngest children. My oldest daughter was okay. She was already living with my mother due to my drug use. That was the day my world came crashing down around me. I went to the program the next day, angry as hell. I found out it was the director who sent CPS to my house for missing the program that Friday. I was on fire. I used that anger to motivate me to prove her wrong.

I discussed my treatment plan with my program counselor that day, and finally, she was able to get me into an in-patient hospital within one week. During the admission process, I had to take a drug test, and it came back NEGATIVE for all controlled substances. This was a 30-day intensive treatment program that was going to save my life. While I was

in-patient, I found out I was pregnant. I had an ultrasound done, and I was told the fetus never developed. I was devastated. It was like as soon as I found out I was pregnant, the pregnancy ended. I had a miscarriage. This was a lot to deal with. Not only did I lose my kids, but I also lost my unborn child. My back was up against the wall. I wanted my life back as the catholic schoolgirl who did not drink or smoke anything. I was so ashamed of myself. It was time to really turn my life around and fight for the life I knew my children, and I deserved. I got focused and started really working the program.

I had a session with my counselor, and we discussed how my life was as a child growing up. I became very emotional because I never realized how much my parent's separation affected me. My dad left home when I was 12 years old. I was angry with my mother and I wanted to make her pay for making my father leave. I lost all trust in her and I no longer believed anything she said. I became defiant, aggressive, and down right disrespectful. I started cutting school and staying out all night. That was a difficult time for me and my siblings. All of our lives had changed forever. My counselor and I realized that this was the root cause of all my pain and my actions. My counselor reached out to my parents to schedule a family session and even though they agreed to come, that session never happened. My insurance would not cover the full 30 days because my drug screen was negative when I was admitted into the hospital, therefore, I had to leave. On the one hand I felt good about that, but on the other hand, I was scared to death. The main thing I took away from my in-patient stay was that PEOPLE, PLACES, AND THINGS would be the cause of my relapse. Those were the main things I had to be aware of and honest about. The day I was discharged was the day that my new life began. I went straight to social services to speak with a case worker in reference to getting my children back. The worker agreed to send my children home the next day. I had to stick with the day program and report in when I was supposed to. The most important thing that I had to do was to stay clean.

The day after being discharged, I went to the program. There were surprised looks on a lot of the faces. During group, we discussed what we did the night before or over the weekend. I had the pleasure of sharing how, after the program, I was going to pick up my kids. The director's wig almost flew off her head. She was so shocked that I was getting my children back. I was on a mission. I was determined to prove everyone, especially her, that this was not the life for me. I left my boyfriend and I started my new life of sobriety with my children.

This process showed me that I deserved all the good things life has to offer me. I woke up every day telling myself, "You can do this. You can turn your life around". Once I let go of the anger and resentment I had towards everyone that I thought was trying to hurt me, I was able to work the program and save my life. My first step was discovering what my WHY was. Why I wanted to transform my life and live. My children were my why. Surrendering was the second step. By surrendering, I choose my life over the drugs and everything else that was attached to it, even my man. I turned my will over to a higher power of my understanding. I let go and let God step in and take control. I had to get out of the way of my recovery. Becoming an open book to set myself free was the most courageous thing I ever had to do.

It was time for school to start so I was transferred to a program closer to my house. My son was able to go to daycare, and my daughter started middle school. I was now able to go to the program and truly focus on me. Things were coming together and started to feel a little more normal. This was a turning point for me. I now realized if I wanted to rediscover who I was I had to make my WHY me. I used the program as the foundation from which I rebuild my life. I connected with individuals who were working the program and winning. I started attending meetings and participating in my recovery. I had an amazing sponsor who took me under her wing and guided me through the 12 steps. When I began to show up and fight for my life, it became clear to me what type of life I wanted. I graduated from the treatment program one year later, and I also celebrated my first year of sobriety on May 4, 2009. At my one-year anniversary, my entire family was there to support me. Looking at the faces of my family told me "Girl, you made the best decision ever, turning your life around. These people really love you and want nothing but the best for you." Letting go of all the anger and resentment allowed me to heal and mend my relationship with my family.

I always had a desire to work in a hospital, so in June 2009, I went to school to become a medical assistant. I graduated in June 2010 as a certified medical assistant with a 4.0 GPA. Before graduating, I was offered a position as an insurance follow-up rep with a physical therapy rehab office in White Plains, NY. Passing this drug test opened a huge door for me. It felt so liberating that I had nothing to worry about. While maintaining a full-time job, I still managed to make my weekly meetings.

9

I would travel and share my story with others, especially the newcomers. I accepted my new lifestyle. No more resentment and no more beating myself up about my past. I would not allow my past to define the woman I was becoming or who I am today.

While rediscovering myself I learned how to love me unconditionally. My recovery was first built around my children, but now I realized I had to do this for me. God first and then me. This was a journey that I would not change any parts to. I now know that I had to go through some storms to get to the life I truly deserve and wanted. I am living my best life ever.

Cleansed and Free, Dear New Me:

Hey Girl, so you are now living drug-free for 11 years and some months now. You continue to fight that disease every day and still manage to choose YOU. You have taken back your life.

Andrea, you are a powerful speaker who have inspired and touched so many lives through your story. You are a bestselling author on the rise. Since 2016, you have been the proud owner of a successful home-based travel business while being an amazing mother to three and grandmother to two. Only through God's grace and mercy are you here today to share this empowering story with others. Continue to grow and remember quitting is not an option.

JOURNAL

AFFIRMATION

Addiction doesn't define me. I own my flaws. Beautifully bruised. but not broken. Gracefully living courageous. determined. and genuinely loving me unconditionally.

April J. Lisbon, Ed.D. is a 20-year veteran school psychologist and parent of a child on the Autism Spectrum. Dr. Lisbon believes in helping families of autistic individuals and other neurodiverse learners identify, clarify, and share their stories without guilt or shame. She believes that by giving families their 'voices' back, they have the power to shift the course of their destinies.

Dr. Lisbon is an empowerment speaker who has spoken on several stages within her local area and various states. She has also appeared as a guest on several podcast shows on iHeart Radio and Apple Podcasts. As an international award-winning author, Dr. Lisbon has authored three books geared towards families raising children with exceptional needs.

She has been seen in the Washington Post, NBC News, Business Insider, Forbes, Autism Parenting Magazine, The TODAY Show, Parenting, Family Circle Magazine, and several other national and international media outlets.

----

www.linkedin.com/in/askdocapril
www.facebook.com/AskDocApril

If The Walls Could Talk

April J. Lisbon, Ed.D

D amn ma, you're back on this f$&8@ table again? And for what? A man that you aren't married to. This joker knows your story, knows your pain, and knows you don't want to get this abortion, but to protect his feelings and emotions, you suppress your own and have this damn needle stuck in your womb again. You ain't nothing and you probably won't be a damn good mother even if you're given the opportunity to do so. What's REALLY good, church girl?

I could have started my story off with something warm and fuzzy like motherhood is one of the greatest gifts ever created. The gift of holding life in your womb for 10 months, nurturing the seed until it becomes a human being. Yet to do so would be unfair to you and me as I would be hiding from the real pain and shame I felt going through these abortions.

17

If I want to come clean and to help you to become set free, I have to give you the real deal and not what makes you feel good. It's who I am and always will be. The only difference is that I have five degrees behind my name and a God that has transformed me.

So, let's get the introductions out of the way as to who I am to date and not who I used to be. My name is Dr. April J. Lisbon and I am an accomplished public school educator, author, national speaker, and mother. Before I was any of these

things, I was a young woman trying to find her way. The ways I took were not always the right path, but they were the paths chosen. I was about that 'thug life'. I was about the fast life and flashing lights with all of the glitter I thought it held. I hated being the good church girl as it was boring to me. I wanted to be like the world and made choices that set me up for a life of self-destruction. These choices brought with it a life of promiscuity, alcohol, and being a part of the drug culture. Definitely not a good look for a young woman brought up in church, but it was indeed a part of my story towards motherhood.

The truth is, I couldn't have a baby by a drug dealer or for anyone else as that wouldn't sit well with my family. My only option was to get the f&*%# abortion and pretend that life was gravy. Oh, but wait. Less than five months later, I was knocked up again. Although we loved each other, having a baby wasn't a good look for two church kids trying to be college educated. Who's going to foot that bill of paying tuition and a baby at the same time? N-O-B-O-D-Y (cues Keith Sweat). Never in a million years did I expect that my experiences at the abortion clinic would alter the trajectory of my future. Nevertheless, there my ass was, legs in the stirrups waiting for it all to happen again.

Then I heard "Are you ready as it will only be a pinch." B*&^$ no I'm not ready, but do I have a choice in the matter? Get the sh#$ over with and stop asking me all of these damn questions I'm not trying to answer right now on this table. Before you know it, the cold needle was stuck into my uterus and the idea of motherhood was released from my body.

God! Why didn't you stop me? I was pissed with God, as he knew my heart and didn't save me. Two abortions before the age of 21. For so many years, in slow motion, I kept hearing in my head–two abortions before the age of 21.

Whose life is this anyway? It's definitely not the life I'd envisioned for myself on my quest of becoming a mother.

I remember vividly when I experienced my first miscarriage. I had visited my ex-lover at the time and the chemistry and magic we shared was beautiful. When I missed my cycle, I was so overjoyed as I felt like the stain and shame of the abortions eight years prior were gone. Those two lines gave me hope that God had not forgotten me and my desire to bring life into the world.

Then one evening, the pain and cramping started. I knew what it was, but I'd hoped that it was a cruel mistake.

When I laid on the hospital table, the doctor said the pregnancy was no longer viable and I would miscarry. I was devastated as I'd turned my life around and felt like God was punishing me because of the first abortion I'd had. I said to myself–I guess it's a life for a life.

I panicked, as I'd feared that if I'd gotten pregnant again, I would miscarry because I'd had two abortions. Less than eight months later I was pregnant again and this time, I conceived my first child.

Less than three years later, I would conceive again. I was so overjoyed. Then it happened again, another miscarriage. What the hell? I was in church and working a steady job. I was married and not sleeping around. I was doing everything by the 'book', but I still miscarried. I said to myself a life for a life as it was not one but two abortions I'd had back in the 90s. We're even now.

Now fast forward five years later. Different time, different place, and a different mate. I had no desire to be pregnant again as I was satisfied with my two. I was two and through.

I was of advanced maternal age the third time around, so the thought of conceiving, let alone being pregnant, seemed like it wasn't in the cards for me. Then like clockwork, I was pregnant again. I remember telling one of my co-workers that day that I was pregnant and how thrilled I was.

Then as the story goes, I miscarried. Miscarried? What do you mean miscarried? Oh, hell no God. This is one too many miscarriages compared to the number of abortions I've had. What the hell man?

I was so angry with God as I felt like he took an innocent life from me without warrant. I had already serves my punishment of the first two abortions, but this go round it was unfair. At that point in life, I didn't want anything to do with God as I felt like he cheated me out of my one last opportunity to be a mother. I was enraged and as I'm typing this now my heart is racing as I remember being in that place and moment in time. But how many of you know that God is a restorer? When the internet told me that it would be hard for me to become pregnant, God changed the channel and gave me one more chance. Like the other two pregnancies, this one stuck and I was blessed to bring forth life again.

Why was this process of birthing life and having babies so hard for me? Mentally and emotionally, I hated answering the question of how many times I'd been pregnant. I despised having to mention the abortions and the miscarriages because I felt like a failure. I felt like I failed myself and my unborn children because I didn't have what it took to carry them. Even after giving birth to my three children, there were times when I would question why the first ones didn't make it. So, every time I'd answer the questions, I would hang my head low and respond. The shame and guilt was unbearable because it rented a space deep within my subconscious for more than 18 years. That's a grown adult.

I'll be honest with you. I thought I'd forgiven myself over the years regarding those abortions. Honestly, I did. It's not like I went to counseling or anything like that. I thought that since I was no longer remembering those events of the past, the pain had been resolved. However, it wasn't until I began writing this chapter that I finally realized that I hadn't released myself from the table.

What do you mean? As I'm writing this chapter to you, there were two revelations that hit me. First, although I physically and financially walked away from the abortion clinic for the second time in less than a years' time span, I'd left my spirit and mind on the table. The second thing that I realized is that I'd lost my ability to trust my decision-making skills. This had rendered me voiceless for so many years to the point where I've stopped trusting the words that I speak concerning me. Hell, I even lost my self-identity. I was more into pleasing people than doing what was best for me.

I then decided that I wanted to shift my own narrative as the one from the past no longer served my present or future. Rather than trying to ignore the pain, I decided I would speak to the pain by any means necessary. I had to become real with me and watch the words that I spoke over my life. I had to move from a place of negative self-talk to positive self-talk on a daily basis. I had to reclaim my voice.

In order to reclaim my voice and subsequently redefine my identity, there are a few things I've chosen not to do in this new season of elevation. I will not allow the words that I speak over my life to abort or miscarry the things that God has called me to do. Assignment cancelled. I will not allow the words that others have spoken, are speaking, or will speak to abort or miscarry what God has destined me to be. Their assignment is

aborted! I will no longer allow my past decisions to hold me hostage in this new season as it has distracted me for far too long. Peace, be gone.

What are you willing to do in this new season? If you are like me, I hope that you are ready to reclaim your voice and redefine your identity as a woman. If you are, look in the mirror and with your right hand, the hand of authority, I want you to speak these words to yourself right now.

Yes, this is a process I had to go through in order to snatch my life back. Right where you are standing, I want you to say these words intentionally:

I'm taking my voice back as I refuse to be enslaved to a table that no longer defines me and knows my name. I'm taking my identity back as I am no longer bound by pleasing people. I'm snatching back my authority as a daughter of the King who has given me the authority to decree and declare life and liberty in me. My past no longer defines me as it no longer knows my name. I am the child of the King. Birthed and clothed in his glory, love, and light. I am getting off the table!

Before I close this chapter, I will say that much has changed since the times of loss for me on my journey towards motherhood. Even when I fell, God still remained true to his promises. Jeremiah 29:11 (NIV) says "For I know the plans I have for you," declares the Lord, "plans to prosper you and not to harm you, plans to give you hope and a future." I am thankful that God knew the plan before I did as with all of the losses, I never fathomed that I would be anyone's mother. Today I am blessed to have three beautiful and healthy children whom I love and adore. God knew the type of children that I needed. It is because of my tribe, as I call them, that I have completed multiple degrees, written several books, been featured in several well-known media prints, and have committed to establishing a prosperous business. I am a kingdom builder who is building a legacy for the children who helped me see the best in me.

In the end, I will never forget the souls that were released from my body as those five seeds were the start of my journey towards motherhood. The greatest lesson I learned throughout this process is to never give up on my dreams, and neither should *you*. God has not forgotten you. Be blessed and GET OFF THE TABLE!

Cleansed and Free, Dear New Me:

April, like so many women, this journey has not been easy by any stretch of the means. There have been times when you've wanted to call it quits and throw in the towel just like every other individual reading this story. Because you chose to fight through the tears and fears and focus on God's written and spoken words EVEN when you disagreed with Him, you now see that it was not meant to harm you but to protect you. Who would have ever thought that you would be sharing this story with the world? Not me, because it was my dirty little secret. Yet, God knew it was time to unapologetically share my truth, less for me and more for those of you reading this chapter right now as you too are ready to release the residue and experience the NEW you.

May I share with you one more thing before I close? I love the new me. Not to say that there won't be obstacles along the way, BUT I have a God that will NEVER fail me because He wants me to succeed. He has commanded me to help other hurting woman through my testimony. Therefore, I accept the challenge. I know that I am officially charged to help other high achieving career women heal and grow through their hurts. I've come to realize that I don't have to follow a script to be the real me and neither do you. Embrace your brilliance and floss your God-given purpose. It's your season to get off of the table and embrace your freedom as it's your birthright from God. Let's go!

JOURNAL

AFFIRMATION

I beautiful inside and out. I am beacon of light. I love who I am flaws and all.

Asia Smith is an inspirational makeup influencer and a spiritual advocate for moms. Her curiosity and innovative spirit led her into opportunities to express her love for makeup while helping moms discover their true inner and outer beauty through her business *Moms Evolve Now*.

The expansion of her love for motherhood widened when she became a mom of two boys. She has been instrumental in helping to provide back to school supply donations, mommy self-care baskets, and hosting mommy meetups in her local community. The success in each project has helped moms combat their self-love, self-care, postpartum depression, and lack of confidence issues.

Instagram @theevolutionofasia
Facebook - Asia Smith
www.momsevolvenow.com

A Secret Relationship with Lust

Asia Smith

My preteen birthday was approaching, and my mom started to ask me what I wanted to do this year, as birthdays had always been a big deal. I decided that I wanted to have the ultimate sleepover. I watched my mom purchase my favorite snacks and pick my best friends up as we prepared for the best night of our lives. My mom had made everything special and set it all out. You would have thought we had two kids and a husband, and this was our girl's night out. I'm partying my socks off, having the time of my life when suddenly I felt a warm liquidly substance run down my leg. I immediately ran to the restroom and saw blood gushing from my panties as I pulled them down. Boy, was I excited!

There was just something about knowing that I had gotten my period that gave me a sense that I had just stepped into true womanhood. I witnessed my peers that were a bit older than me complain about the stomach cramps. Despite their complaints, I still was eager to see what it all was about. It's crazy that our body longs for the things that aren't good for us, knowing that we will have to fight through the process in order to receive our healing. I was told what to do to stop the blood flow, but I wasn't warned of the sexual hormones that would begin to flow. We all hear the typical black mom sermon "don't bring no babies in my house", but I wish I would have heard the sermon that I would start to feel this sensation go through my body at times that would give me chills and make me feel as though I no longer had control. As my menstrual came and went, I started to become in tune with my body. The feelings that were arising caused my curiosity to start to itch at me like a mosquito bite. The overflow of hormones was overwhelming me and I didn't know who to vent these emotions to except in my diary.

One night after eating dinner, I decided to knock out early. I woke up in the middle of the night and decided to watch an old classic that was being shown on HBO, "Pretty In Pink". As the credentials were scrolling on the television screen, a preview of what's coming next appeared showing two women kissing. I knew that it was wrong to watch but my eyes were glued as if it was my favorite after school cartoon. The hairs on my arm began to rise up and at the moment I had let the spirit of homosexuality not just visit me, but it stayed until I was 22 years old. I eventually went to sleep and didn't think much more of it until the next night and my curiousness began to want to see more and more. Quickly I had become anxious to watch networks showcase two women making out and indulging into each other's flesh. At school, when the young boys mentioned two women making out, they made it seem as if it was a harmless act. They had no clue that they were confirming what I thought was the newfound likeness of myself. This attraction was hidden for years until I reached high school, began to drive on my own and hang out with my friends. One warm Saturday in the late evening, my friend shot me a text and said they were having a get together. They said it was nothing too serious, just few of them having a good time and I was welcomed to come.

Of course, as a no brainer I replied that I was on my way and I just knew it was going to be a great time. The night passed on as the girls and I twerked and moved to the music; feeling the alcohol kick in made us even more relaxed. I decided to take a smoke break with my friend as we were smoking and inhaling the Black & Mild, we began to talk about our feelings. Most of the conversation was about how no one truly understood us and then she mentioned that she was dating a female. My heart started to race. As you can imagine, I was thinking "It's no way this chick knows my secret." She proceeded to go into more detail about how she had sex with the girl, and she had to cut it off because it was becoming too serious. My armpits are beginning to sweat as I wondered "should I tell her my secret?" We headed back into the party, and I had become entirely too wasted to even make it home. The friend who was having the party offered to let me stay the night and I shared a huge pallet on the floor with the friend who I shared the Black & Mild with. Little did I know that it was a complete set up from the enemy as a chance to test the waters. I laid beside her and began to let the alcohol release my secrets on how I was attracted to women as well.

The next morning, I woke up looking at my friend's face. I glanced down and noticed all of my clothes were off and I immediately began to regret what I allowed happen throughout the night. I was so disappointed in myself that I had really let the sensation overtake me. I didn't know how to feel about it so I did what I assumed was best and I never mentioned it to anybody. My high school days became more traumatizing as the girls would bully me because of my beauty and the guys secretly lusted after my figure. I still didn't know who I was deep inside, especially after feeling the rejection from my father not being fully present. I needed to feel wanted and when I didn't, I knew how to get it at whatever cost.

Life began to unravel and before I knew it, I was married at twenty with my first baby boy. My truth was forcing itself to appear, not only in front of me, but also in front of my husband. When we would have sex, thoughts of having sex with another woman began to rise up in me like a hidden story that was never told by the writer. I pushed off and rebuked it because I knew from a Holiness Apostolic Church perspective, the lustful spirit that was dwelling in me would never see God's face in peace. I didn't understand how this feeling could still be sitting in me despite the fact that I went to church regularly and believed that Jesus died for my sins. What was wrong with me? The question continually ran through my head, "what if I really did like the other sex?" As I went to work each day, my role as a trainee was changing and we had to walk the bottom floor of the call center to view our new assigned seats. When I saw her, I knew she wanted me and I secretly wanted her. I had the picture-perfect lifestyle, but due to the attention that I was not receiving at home, I was unfulfilled. I became frustrated and before I knew it, she and I were spending time indulging into each other's sexual desires. Then, one night I was so intoxicated my lips were numb and when I woke up the next day, what I thought was a hangover was morning sickness from my second baby boy. When I saw that big positive appear on the pregnancy test, immediately I knew God was cutting it all off. I fell to my knees as the tears began to fall. I yelled out "NOOOO I CAN'T DO THIS"! I knew I was living a double life and even after fulfilling every desire, I had no peace and I wanted out, but not like this. I became angry with God and asked him how in the world could I be a mom of two kids? He spoke to me so clearly and said, "that's enough, no more". In that moment I surrendered my mind, body, and soul to God. It took some time to let go of the entanglement that sprouted between me and this girl, but I knew I wanted better for myself which was a peace of mind.

Once I accepted who I was and what I had battled with for many years, I fell to my knees and recommitted my life back to Christ. I asked Him to wash away my sins and forgive me for the trespasses that invaded my mental privacy. The decision wasn't based on culture or religion but me knowing for myself that God sent his own son to take care of a secret that was keeping me in bondage. Had I not recommitted my life to Him, I would still be holding a lustful spirit that is not of God. I detoxed from the drugs, alcohol, and the sexual identity that came along with the desire to please my flesh and feel wanted.

My second son was my saving grace and now I work daily in my ministry to encourage other moms to become new in Christ. I realized that God knew each imperfection and because of his love for me, he offered me a do over. Instead of me aborting it, Jesus accepted it because the life full of lies and secrets that I was living was not aligned with who he had called me to be. I was no longer bound, feeling that there was no way out. I had a real moment with God and let him know that I couldn't get rid of those feelings that laid dormant inside of my mind and body. Ultimately, it made me go deeper into finding out what God called me and who he designed me to be. The urge will always be there, but the self-control to say no to Satan's wicked devices empowers me every day to become the best me I could possibly be in the eyes of the Lord.

Cleansed and Free, Dear New Me:

Do you remember when you used to pray for God to take you off this earth? Do you remember when you just wanted one person to love you the way your heart desired? Now look at you! Every day you wake up feeling God's presence and learning more about how much He loves and values you. The weight that you were carrying was too heavy and you've finally released the secrets that were holding you back from becoming who God has called you to be -- which is pure greatness. Listen, you better keep evolving! It's no turning back now!

JOURNAL

AFFIRMATION

New Life, new beginnings turning leaves over to the new you, spring up and move forward!

Benita Williams, or Ms. B as many calls her, is a Life Coach, Speaker and Author who is strongly committed to supporting individuals of all ages deal with severe life stressors.

Ms. B's stressors go back to her being an only child who then loses her mother as a young adolescent.

Ms. B assists clients to heal from life stressors that can cause traumatic experiences leading to ineffectual relationships. Her clients develop healthy perceptions of self, allowing them to embrace relationships that are peaceful, complete and safe.

Ms. B's background includes twenty years working with students in crisis. Her responsibilities were to de-escalate student crises and work intensively with students to develop alternative behaviors. Her formal education includes a BA in Psychology.

To schedule a speaking engagement, please contact Benita Williams, Inc at benitatwilliams40@gmail.com
***or* https://www.facebook.com/benita.williamssmith**

Addicted to The Unknown

Benita Williams

To some, being an only child is a good thing. There are material benefits and the feeling of being equally loved by both parents. To me, however, it was the source of my attachment issues.

My attachment concerns manifested when my mother passed away. Her passing opened a gateway for the devil to use to torment me with feelings of loneliness. It pushed me to make decisions in a weary state of mind without trusting or consulting with God. My state of mind had me running into enemy territory. I would agree with all the lies the enemy told me just to be accepted and not feel alone. I had no understanding that this was the appointed time God was using to raise me into the woman he wanted me to be.

In the month of my mother's death, I received confirmation that I was pregnant. I was 17 years old and decided to keep the child. I needed someone else to be close to me. I was not deterred by the fact that I was a young lady who knew nothing about raising a child, was not married, nor had I received my degree. I was afraid of being alone, and that led me to keep my child. By the way, I thought having a fear of being alone was normal.

I found myself going through life allowing myself to be connected to people in any manner. I wanted to feel like I had friends/family, and I wanted the assurance of not being alone. During my first long-term relationship, I had two children. We were a young couple and I accepted the gradual detachment of this relationship by replacing it with another one. After the first failed relationship, the second one also failed, and then came a third unsuccessful relationship. I found myself in a fourth relationship, agreeing to bring forth another child hoping to live life happily ever after as a family. I hadn't realized that I hadn't give myself time to heal from the previous failed relationships. This relationship filled a void while the feeling misled me to believe it was so right, yet so different.

After the birth of my daughter, I began to feel like this partnership was leading to no peace in my life. My mind, my body and my soul felt like I had sacrificed possible happiness for a feeling called pain. Though I knew this pain was not constructive, I didn't realize that I was verbally, then mentally abused. The verbal abuse from this man I envisioned to be my soul mate began to flow like a river. Everything I thought I could do to lessen the abuse only made things worse.

I felt if I went back to school to achieve my BA degree that this man would see my worth on an upgraded level -- but no. Instead, he would ridicule me for not using the degree once I achieved that goal. He often reminded me that if it weren't for him watching our daughter, I wouldn't be able to accomplish anything. Although I didn't utilize my degree immediately, he never valued the fact that I was employed by a company where I had 15 years of service. I could retire today or tomorrow because I was a woman who had enough years to collect my retirement before the required age.

It wasn't long after the verbal abuse began that the mental abuse exposed itself in greater measure. The man I thought I would live the rest of my life with began to secretly step out of the relationship physically. The disrespect of that deception was so disgraceful and humiliating. I was so ashamed of myself for still loving him. The very first infidelity I witnessed should have allowed me to walk away from the relationship with my self-respect intact.

I accommodated my spouse like a wife should. I would pack his lunch for him to take to work. I would research directions for him when he had to go to an unfamiliar site location. One night I was getting myself ready for bed after cleaning up. We talked for a few minutes on the phone as we always did, but something just didn't feel right about the conversation. I began to feel restless with myself, and it wasn't from being 9 months pregnant with our son. It was a different feeling, one that I had been feeling for an exceptionally long time but just was not able to put an explanation to it. I called my spouse numerous times in hopes of him easing the feeling that I had but I received no response. I got in my car with my 3-

year-old daughter and our little Yorkie deciding to ease my own curiosities. Upon arrival at the site, I witnessed the love of my life, with whom I was having our second child, engaged in a sexual act on the hood of a car.

By this time, I was experiencing a second level of abuse. I was so numb I recall still wanting to stay in this relationship. I also remember wondering what would come next--physical abuse? That could be no worse than what I already was experiencing. I continued to stay with my spouse, slapping a band-aid on every disappointment that I was confronted with in hopes that it would show him that I remained loyal even though he did not. Today I would say that I became a slave to the

41

abuse. I sacrificed my happiness for many years just so the outsiders who entertained my spouse would know I was not going anywhere. I allowed my soul to be broken into pieces. I would get so worked up about issues that had no importance at all that it had a noticeably negative effect on me and those around me. My patience with my children was way below minimal. I would remind my kids that it was always me doing what was required to rear them into productive citizens as if it were their fault. I would mention how unfair it was that their father did not physically do his Father/Daddy duties. The state of mind their father projected at this time was that if he provided financially, then he was taking care of his children.

My children saw me always crying and asked what was wrong until they finally stopped asking. They knew it was due to their dad's lack of involvement and the continuous verbal disrespect he directed toward me even in front of the children. My friends of over 18 years would try to remind me how beautiful I was inside and out. They said that I didn't deserve to be treated as I was being treated. I listened, knowing that it was my choice whether I would apply the advice offered. The spirit that had my mind in captivity would tell me to evaluate the fact of whether they were in a relationship or not. I had to do this before I entertained even a mustard seed of their truth with regard to my situation.

Most of my time was spent at work, and my coworkers/family were also affected by what was transpiring in my life. They knew if I wasn't that happy, vibrant individual at work, something must be wrong. There were some colleagues I would share my story with. They tried to encourage me to not tolerate anything that was not conducive to my well-being as a woman. I needed and appreciated all the love that was given to me by colleagues and students whom themselves had dealt with worse trauma than I could ever imagine. I was able to help them cope with their issues but was so unsuccessful with my own. Why wasn't I enough as a woman, as the mother of this man's children? Why was my partner choosing females/friends that brought no value to his life? Why was I still in love with a man that was treating me less than the Queen that I am? Why couldn't I let go when confronted by all the reasons I should leave this man? Why was I feeling like I was not worthy enough to have a man love me for me and totally commit to me and his family? Is there something wrong with me? Am I crazy? That's when I received my rebirth. I realized I had been filling my voids with my own choices. I had been leaning on my own understanding of how to deal with my life. I decided I had enough of sacrificing myself, of allowing my life to go around in circles. I wanted to walk a straight path. My circumstances would drive me crazy if I did not detach myself from them.

Instead of questioning my life experiences, I needed to change them. I had to invite God into my life as my Lord and Savior and commit to living life according to His will. I had to start by allowing God to show me what builds me up and does not destroy me. As self-reflection was applied, things began to become much clearer to me. I was unknowingly dealing with an addiction.

I was addicted to everything that connected me to the companionship of a man who clearly was toxic to me. I had to confront all the things that kept me in captivity. I spoke against everything that made me feel powerless or hopeless and replaced it with thinking differently about myself. I spoke positive affirmations daily to myself like (Jeremiah 1:5) adapting the quote to fit my need:

Before you formed me (Benita Williams) in the womb God, you knew me, and before I was born, you consecrated me. You appointed me (Benita) to do all things because you knew I was the one for the assignment. I am fearfully and wonderfully made to win. Your works are wonderful. I know full well that I will win in my FINANCES, in my CAREER, I will win MENTALLY, EMOTIONALLY, and PHYSICALLY. I will win FAMILY WISE and in everything I do, I will win. With God before me, who can be against me"?

I live daily, going through the process of becoming whole with fasting and prayer (2 Corinthians 4:16-17). I am no longer willing to be loyal to anyone who, like I was, may not be loyal to themselves. I focus on being obedient to God and what He projects to my inward parts (Proverbs 20:27).

My mind, body and soul became liberated the moment I stopped worrying and "Let Go and Let God." I was once afraid of being alone, but now I receive peace in my time of loneliness. I have learned that in those lonely moments, God sees, understands and listens to every concern that touches my life. Trusting God and the process has shown me there is more "Can" in me than Can't. My life shall forever reflect that all that transpired was a process making me the Extraordinary Woman I am.

Cleansed and Free, Dear New Me:

The shift that was needed to get your mind to understand all that was required was not easy and you are still evolving. I am proud of you for being brave enough to wipe the cluster from your eyes to see and receive the changes that were needed. The journey of newness that will permeate your life if you stay obedient to trust, and walk in faith will alter your life dramatically for good. New me, don't be ashamed of the obstacles that you may encounter; take them all as learning experiences and continue to grow.

JOURNAL

AFFIRMATION

Healing the wounds, forgiving the heart, and overcoming the shame. The pain is mine to release in time as I love myself again.

Celeste Pinckney
Grief Coach, Author and Speaker has a heart for all people. It has been her mission to care for, offer hope, and spread inspiration to those in need. She retired from the Federal government in 2014 as an investigator for the Office of Personnel Management.

She is a three-time Amazon bestselling co-author in the books, *Your Wings Were Ready But My Heart Was Not, Diary of a People Pleaser, and I Told the Storm.* She is also the CEO of UniquelyMee (an e- commerce business).

True to her life mission, in the very near future, she will be launching a brand-new Grief and Bereavement Service business to assist those individuals in our society who need a compassionate caring friend to lend a helping hand.

Celeste can be reached at:
Celeste.pinckney@yahoo.com
info@celestepinckney.com

The Healing Jar

Celeste Pinkney

I am reminded of the famous children's bedtime prayer: "Now I lay me down to sleep. I pray the Lord my soul to keep. If I should die before I wake, I pray to God my soul to take."

Well, the day has come, and I am awake. I have my YES, a brand-new start!

Hey, mind, I feel angry and so beat up. When I look in my bathroom mirror, I can't see me. All I see is scar after scar after scar and I don't even have a big jar to drop all of my bruises into. Truth be told, I CAN'T say I don't know how I got here. Most of my life, I was afraid of mainly two words: DEATH and the FEAR—specifically, the fear of being alone. I was the one who needed the validation of people, mainly men, and got lost in me.

Because I felt lost and so alone all my life, I just wanted to be accepted and for someone to love and respect me. Although my parents and family gave me love, I was the one looking for love "with the wrong men." Growing up, I was the shy one, the one who would sit and listen to everyone else conversing but not say a word. I had so many pinned up emotions and pain, but in 2014, all of my grief came to the surface and "hit the fan." The death of my mother and those nasty physical relationships that I had with badly, beaten down, bruised men who only wanted me for sex were a turning point in my life. I had to get help.

It's funny how the worst day of my life is turning into the best days of my life.

I can't even count the years that I allowed things to happen to me.

I wasn't allowed to date until I was 17 years old, so I felt like a late bloomer. I guess I really thought I was missing out on something. HA! HA! HA!

Fast forward, and the days after 17 were a mess. That's when I thought I was doing the "dang" thing. I married at the age of 19, thinking I was grown, but it ended after two years. I married again at age 25, thinking I was healed. I was carrying a bag full of scars that included a lack of self-love and self-worth that was getting in my way. Both of these marriages were abusive, and after my second marriage, my life began to spiral downwards. There was man after man after man. I was guilty until proven innocent. My daughter still tells me to this day that back in the day, I thought I was the "Queen Bee." Ironically, my daughter and I can still laugh about these old times. This may offend some but can be real to others. The truth is, EVERYONE has a past.

It's funny how the worst day of my life is turning into the best days of my life.

Hey, mind, it's okay to be alone. I was now in the 20th century, and I kept making the same old mistakes. Studying the Word of God, going to church, professing Christ, and no goodness. But I know better.

I called myself taking a break from men, but oh, how that temptation sets in. And guess what? Shortly after that, I met this fine man. He was shy and very private. He was somewhat short (but that's okay with me), well-dressed, groomed to a tee, intelligent, muscular, comes from a prominent family, but was a drunk. I wanted to meet this man so badly, so a friend of mine introduced me to him. I had no idea at the time that he was an alcoholic. We would talk on the phone a little but not enough to get any valuable information.

On our first date, Mr. A and I were supposed to go out, but when he came to pick me up, it turned into a house date. The second date turned into a house date too, which included carryout food and led to the bedroom. He would drink until all he could do was tiptoe. Every date from then on turned into watching television, eating, and "You Know" in my Ice Cube voice. Sex was all he wanted. We rarely kissed or showed any signs of affection. We did this for years. As far back as I can remember, we only went out socially twice, but guess what happened? He packed up, left, and moved to another state with another woman without even telling me. I found out through the grapevine. He left to be with her, thinking he would build a family, but it didn't work.

Remember, I said we did this for years and years. Yes, he came back, and who does he call? Me!

We were back together again. This time the routine changed a little. We would go from either my house or his house. I would spend the night and get up to leave the very next day, until the next time.

I would end up getting tired of this foolishness, and the breakup would occur (It's time to keep track).

Back to Being Alone.

It's funny how the worst day of my life is turning into the best days of my life.

Hey mind, it is now 2001? It seems like history is repeating itself, but the only difference this time is that I understand what is happening to me. It seems like it was just yesterday or like last week that I laid in my bed with my eyes closed, repenting to God and asking for forgiveness.

Here we go again! This time I met this man on my own. I tried to ignore him when he kept coming on to me, but he was persistent so I gave in. It started out with great phone conversations and meetups in local areas. We realized that we had common interests and family ties. He would come over and try to shower me with gifts. Things were going great. I had taken a long break from dating anyone, had accomplished goals that I never dreamed of completing, finished counseling, and was moving on with my life. Then the thing I dreaded happened. I started catching him in lie after lie, so I decided to say goodbye.

I wasn't going to put up with any more garbage. However, one day he came to visit unexpectedly, and on that day, he must have been feeling his oats. When I opened the door, I told him to leave and that he was not getting in, but he forced his way through the door. He kept trying to hug and kiss me, but I kept pushing him away. We went back and forth--- back and forth. I even tried pulling him back towards the front door. He just kept trying to justify his lying, but I was not having it. So, all of a sudden, he told me he had to go to the bathroom. I told him after that he had to go. When he came out of the bathroom, he did not return. I went looking for him, and he was in my bedroom---butt naked. I was so furious by now! I was raising my voice and pulling on him to get out of my bed. He got one good grip, and I was in my bed fighting for life.

Consequently, I trembled. It was a tremble you could feel with just a touch. I was trying to use all of my strength to push him off of me. I was using my hands when they were free and trying to get my legs free. He was big and strong, and as I laid in my bed, he forcibly started touching and feeling on me abruptly. I was lying there in silence, praying, "God Forgive Me." The force of the kissing and caressing made me weep. My eyes were watered from crying, my voice quivered, and I was at a loss for words. He took the strength of his legs to force my legs open, and "it was on." I was fighting trying to push him off of me, but he wouldn't stop. He was acting like a mad man by now and even more determined. He couldn't get a full erection, so he began to lick and lick. It hurt so badly. I finally was able to get him off of me, and I told him he raped me. He replied, "NO, I'm just greedy and I needed some." I tried my best to maintain my composure but couldn't.

In my mind, I am saying, "How is this happening to me again?" I entered into this new dating relationship with the notion of "he is okay" because of what I observed from a few of his family members. The sad part about it is he saw no wrong in what he'd done. I had to forgive myself and forgive him.

Back to therapy, I go.

Back to being alone.

It's funny how the worst day of my life is turning into the best days of my life.

Hey mind, why do I keep going back to (A) who is not looking for what you are seeking? How could I let myself, after all these years, be with a man I know nothing about? I know where he lives, what kind of cars he drives, what kind of job he does, the names of his family members, the names of a few of his friends and that's all. I never met anyone associated with him, yet he has met my whole immediate family. I have talked until I turned blue in the face explaining to him that I am a good woman and have so much to offer. He agrees, but somehow we have not taken this relationship to the next level after more than 15 years. I explain to him that I must not be the one. All he does is give excuses. Time waits for no one, but I keep dragging myself back to him.

Then the pattern changed a little. I asked him to take me out for my birthday, and he did. I bet you can figure out the rest! Month after month, it was the same old tune. Until one day, I get the okay from him that I can start coming over anytime. Wow...that had never happened!

By the time he tells me this, I am sick and tired of the sick and tired. I started digging deep within myself to uncover those nasty scars that I carried for so long. I focused on going to counseling and also rededicated my life to God. I also started setting boundaries and chose to really change my life.

But my thought was, "I am not getting any younger."

By now, a change is occurring in him and guess who is not included. He is acting more bold and extra arrogant. He is starting to hang out with a friend who has a girlfriend. When they go out, her girlfriends also come. I tell you, it became ugly. The disrespect really started to show because I had started changing and wasn't going to waste my precious time anymore. He stooped so low as to tell me the girls wanted his D!#?, so I better come and get it. That was it. I'd had enough, so I ended it.

It's funny how the worst day of my life is turning into the best days of my life.

Well, Pandora (me) must have shut the door halfway.

Thinking that Mr. (A) and I were just friends, no benefits, I called him because I was in the process of opening up an e-commerce store. I wanted him to support it and pass the information along to others. I was sadly mistaken. There was one text after another. I would try explaining why I ended the relationship, and he would say he understood but would blame me for trying to force him into a relationship. This went on and on. Finally, he told me he understood, but in the next second, he was sexting me his private parts. Then he would come back with I'm sorry in the next sentence and tell me good luck on finding a good man like him.

On that day, it was my last time, and I mean THE last time ever having anything with him. He made me lose my religion for a minute. He realized I was finally done, so he went off on me. He told me I was slow and called me an old ass. Then he told me his friends said he was wasting his time on me. His family told him he didn't need to be with someone desperate. Then he put the icing on the cake with F##K, and it just went on and on. I came back with two choice words that were not nice. F##K you...Period!!! I blocked him from calling me and got rid of any of his contact information. It would have made your head spin. That episode was so hurtful because that was the last person I expected to come at me like that. I had to ask for God's forgiveness, forgive myself, and forgive him.

One more scar that I can leave and seal tight in my jar. It's funny how the worst day of my life is turning into the best days of my life

From this day forth, I will continue to pray, fast, and seek God's face. I will remember that I am the Prize. I will remember that my boundaries are not negotiable. This will enable me to hear and see clearer to help and inspire others.

I learned how to say "Yes" to me and "No" to others.

It doesn't take a man to make you happy and complete.

It is okay to be alone.

Sex can come with a price.

It's okay to seek help.

Cleansed and Free, Dear New Me:

So today, May 2020, My Dear New Me! I am so proud of you. With the help of God, you have healed bruises and then sealed them into your jar of scars. Today is your day of freedom. The end of one life and the beginning of a new one. I am proud of you, you truly love yourself, and know your worth. A day where your past no longer haunts you. A day where you truly know what you expect of a man. A day where you can look clearly in your mirror and smile and say, "Girl You Got This." A day that you will never ever be the same.

JOURNAL

AFFIRMATION

Standing on the pain of my faded scars.
My strength restored and empty jars.
Beautifully flawed and embracing it all.
I am worthy!

Charmaine Roots Castillo is an author, model, editor and inspirational storyteller. At the age of 63, she became a first-time published author sharing the story of her son's murder in her first book "Who Killed My Son: A Mother's Wait for Justice". She then went on to become a two-time best-selling author in her collaboration in the anthology "Soulful Prayers: The Power of Intentional Communication with God, Volumes 1 and 2.

Having 40+ years' experience as a legal assistant, and being inspired by her son's death to live life to the fullest, Charmaine formed the company, The LaFondé Experience, LLC, to showcase her skills as a writer, editor, model and speaker. She was a featured model for *Basic Hair Care*, and her story was also featured in Today's Purpose Woman Magazine. Charmaine is an avid bowler and tennis player who's mantra is "You are never too old to pursue your dreams."

Connect with her at: LaFonde56@gmail.com or www.CharmaineCastillo.com

The Courage To Speak

Charmaine Roots Castillo

I dreaded the moment that was about to unfold. I slowly walked towards the front door of the house and had an eerie feeling in the pit of my stomach as I stepped onto the porch. As I unlocked the door and stepped into the foyer, my knees buckled a little bit. I had barely taken a step inside when an overwhelming odor took my breath away. It smelled like 500 pounds of rotting meat that had been left in the scorching sun for days. I had never smelled anything as horrendous as the stench of a rotted corpse and it is a smell that I will never forget. The moving team rushed in behind me and immediately began opening all of the windows in the now unoccupied duplex.

I regained my composure and walked down the hallway to the bedroom. From the doorway, I peeped in and caught a glimpse of the blood-soaked mattress. The detective arrived and began to remove multiple guns and boxes of ammunition from the pantry where they were stored. He looked at me, now a widow and a single parent, with compassion in his eyes and slowly shook his head. That was my reality. After three years of being trapped in a marriage that was like a prison of hell, I stood in the middle of that bedroom, reflecting on the fact that I was finally free.

I was too ashamed for anyone to know what a traumatic life I had been living, but little did they know what I had lived through. How in the world did I end up married to him in the first place? I was ashamed of the decision that I had made, and I wore a mask to hide the secret pain that I lived with every day of my life. I was too ashamed to talk about it to anyone, so I suffered in silence.

I lived with a fear of rejection and desperately wanted to be accepted. I lost my voice in the process.

How often do we live our lives based on what other people will think about us? How often do we make decisions based on what we think will make others happy, when deep down inside we know that we are compromising our own happiness? How often do we say yes when we want to say no? How often do we make decisions that we regret, only to feel trapped by our own choices? These were some of the mistakes that I made early on in my life, but by God's grace and mercy I have been able to rebuild my life based on his purpose and plan. I have been able to recover from a life that had been full of not so wise choices and am well on my way to living my best life because I have lived and learned. I am now happy to be living a life that has shifted for the better – I made that choice to shift.

When I was in my late teens, my world shifted for the worst when I walked in on my high school sweetheart having sex with someone else. My heart was broken, my mind was numb, and my self-esteem was crushed. The pain of that rejection crippled me and left me asking "What did I do wrong?"

My self-worth was challenged based on the misdeeds of someone else, but I did not take the time to heal from that assault on my self-worth. My mother tried to console me when she said that someone else would come along, so six months later as I was riding the bus to work, our eyes locked as he stepped onto the bus. I was still feeling the pain of rejection, betrayal, and a broken heart, but when he sat down beside me and asked my name, I felt pretty again – I felt desirable. I even thought "maybe I'm not damaged goods after all."

He had a quiet gentleman-like demeanor and I was flattered. My relationship mindset had been formulated based on the golden rule and I believed that if I treated others as I would have them treat me, I would be rewarded in-kind. I was hopeful that my faith in men would be restored, so I forged on, ignoring the voice of my conscious and the nagging sense that something was not quite right in this budding new relationship.

The more time we spent together, the more I noticed behavior that was a little bit bothersome -- he expressed anger towards me when I shared an opinion that he didn't agree with. I was a lover of peace and always leaned in the direction of peace, so for the sake of peace, I remained quiet -- not defending my stance. I did not realize at the time that I was choosing to surrender my voice in order to be accepted. I chose to compromise my core beliefs just to be with someone who was not right for me. I chose not to rock the boat. . . I sat there silently hoping that the storm would pass. Four months into that relationship, at the tender age of 20, I married him.

Almost immediately, things began to turn dark as I found myself isolated from my family and friends. I was constantly berated and belittled. His words were sharp and cut like a knife. My already fragile self-esteem was smashed under the weight of his condescending words. He attacked my intelligence and spoke to me as if I were a child. He was unable or unwilling to acknowledge my feelings and systematically disqualified them. I began to disqualify myself.

Have you ever reconsidered your worth based on someone else's perception of you? I was humiliated and too afraid to speak up to defend myself. I cowered in silence as he punched holes in walls and doors with his fists whenever he was frustrated. He was always frustrated. Every move that I made was under constant scrutiny – whether I was talking on the phone to a friend or family member or telling a complete stranger who asked me, what the time was. I became paralyzed by the fear of not pleasing him. This was not how I wanted to live, but I was too afraid to say anything to anyone. I hid from the world what I was experiencing behind closed doors. I stifled my emotions in his presence and used the shower as my secret place to cry.

I buried myself in my career, which had become my safe haven. There I found acceptance and there my worth was acknowledged and appreciated. I felt validated and for a few hours a day, I felt a sense of normalcy.

Living in such a volatile environment was beginning to take a toll on me. Desperate for help, I scheduled a secret meeting with my pastor to share what I was living through. What I hoped would be a pathway to relief, ended up as a religious diatribe against divorce. Really? Was the legalism of this church actually being put in front of the emotional and physical well-being of my child and me? Rules over relationship? As I drove back to the hell that I called home, I felt that I was facing a literal death. I was disappointed that what I received as counsel was a legalistic view of marriage. I felt hopelessly trapped.

When I got home, I decided that if it was meant for me to continue to suffer in such a toxic marriage, I would kill myself. One day, when I was home alone, I swallowed a handful of anti-depressant pills, hoping to never wake up on this side of heaven. I felt like an utter failure when I did wake up. Have you ever been disappointed to wake up? I considered the notion that my son, who was 3 years old at the time, just might need his mother. Still, after enduring another year of a more intense and volatile atmosphere, I laid aside my motherly instincts and contemplated another attempt to end my life. As I applied pressure to the trigger, my quest to end my life I was interrupted by a vision that I had of my mother walking in and finding me dead. As soon as I understood what that vision meant, I moved the gun away from my temple and sobbed profusely as I cried out to the only one who could save me – "God!! I can't live this way -- please help me!"

The more volatile my husband became, the more guns he bought. His animosity for people in general was more profusely pronounced and he began to stockpile ammunition and gun powder in preparation for what he called the "race war". One night he forced a gun into my hand and pleaded with me to shoot him. I wanted to, but I was afraid that he would not die. I often fell asleep to the sound of him cleaning guns, I felt unsafe and afraid – I no longer wanted to live my life in fear.

One day I had taken a day off from work and I had time to sit and think. I thought about my life and I began to think about me. I thought about the dreams that I once had envisioned of being a wife and raising a family. I thought about how I grew up as a little girl in a loving home environment and how far away I was from those dreams. I thought about my son and how important it was for him to have a mother that was happy and healthy.

I realized that my dreams were still attainable, and I remember hearing my mother say, "you can do bad all by yourself." Sitting there in that moment, I was doing bad, but I wanted to make a change. It was in that moment of thought that I made my first step towards freedom – I made a decision. My mindset shifted from "accept what is" to "my life matters and I don't have to accept this". I made a decision to remove myself from that toxic environment so that I could breathe again. As soon as I made a decision to make a change in my life, I felt totally refreshed and as I began to make an exit plan, I felt courage arising within me. Hope became alive and I was on my way. My first steps to freedom were:

Change your mindset and then make a decision to change your life.

After I made that decision to reclaim my life, my next steps were to make and execute a plan. The courage that I needed to do what needed to be done was already within me. I used my lunch hour to fill out an

67

application for an apartment, and when it was approved, I loaded up my trunk with my clothes, picked up my son from daycare and went directly to that empty apartment – my safe house.

I was not surprised when he showed up at my door, and I was not surprised when he pulled out a gun and begged me to shoot him, again. I did not anticipate that I would be violated at gunpoint. Yes, I was raped by my husband. After he left, I cried in the shower as I attempted to wash his filth off of me. That was the last time that I saw him alive.

Two weeks later, sitting in my empty apartment, a detective showed up at my door to give me the news that my husband's body was found – dead from a self-inflicted gunshot wound to the head. I cried tears of relief. It's over!!

It has been said that experience is the best teacher, but I beg to differ. I believe that the best teacher is one who has lived the experience and has acquired the wisdom to impart to others on how they can avoid the pitfalls altogether. As I share some of the lessons that I learned, it is my desire that you avoid the mistakes that I made and align more swiftly with your destiny.

Don't ever compromise what you believe in order to please other people. Know how valuable you are and never allow anyone to diminish your value by the way that they treat you. Respect yourself if you expect others to respect you. You are already accepted by God and you need no other acceptance.

I am a survivor who has overcome rejection, betrayal, shame, rape, and the fear of man that caused me to lose my voice. After I made a decision to choose life on my terms, I embarked on a journey of healing. I had to slowly rebuild what had been torn asunder on the inside of me. I had to learn to love myself again. When I began to see myself the way that God saw me, my life shifted for the better.

No matter where you are in your life right now, it is never too late to begin to live your dream. You have the power within you to choose the life that you want and not make excuses for staying in a place that does not fulfill you. As I began to elevate my thinking, I could hear the voice of my mother exhorting me to "shoot for the moon -- if you miss you will land amongst the stars."

It has been a long journey to break free from the spirit of fear that held me captive for so long and it has been a long journey for me to finally find my voice again. I am a light that will not be hidden under a bushel and now I have a reason to

smile. I am excited for what is ahead for me and for those who are closest to me. As I boldly step into my next level of living, I am thrilled to be able to dance into my future cleansed and free!!

Cleansed and Free, Dear New Me:

You are courageous. You are loved and you are a woman of great worth. You are fearfully and wonderfully made, and your wrong decisions do not define who you are. Don't be afraid to boldly challenge what you feel is wrong and fear NO ONE. You are accepted by the one who loves you most -- the Lord your God, and you do not need the approval of anyone else. You are the righteousness of Christ. Now that you have reclaimed your voice, use it to help others.

JOURNAL

AFFIRMATION

Skillfully I speak with confidence and style. My voice is crafted as a divine weapon to release the captives.

Harriet Rogers Pridgen was born and
raised in the city of Philadelphia, Pennsylvania. She graduated from South Philadelphia High School. Harriet later moved to Burgaw, North Carolina, where she worked for the North Carolina Housing Authority for thirteen years. After leaving the housing authority, she became a North Carolina Correctional Officer of eighteen years retiring on January 1st, 2020.

As of 2013 she has served as an advocate for abused and neglected children through the North Carolina Guardian Ad Litem Program. She's also a licensed preacher with multiple certificates in ministry, leadership training, and substance abuse training, She also received her associate degree in Biblical Studies. Harriet is currently employed as an Environmental Service Assistant at New Hanover Regional Medical Center. A devote Christian, a wife, a mother, and a grandmother. It is her ultimate desire to open a transitional house for low risk offenders.

Contact
Email: harrietprdgn1@gmail.com
https://www.facebook.com/hrogerspridgen

It's My Anniversary

Harriet Rogers Pridgen

My third wedding anniversary was fast approaching and I couldn't wait for that day to come. I felt so much excitement because finally, we had reached a point of being on one accord. I was planning every detail of how we would celebrate our love for each other, but to my surprise, his plans were much different from mine.

I walked into the room where he was to share the anniversary plans with him and I was devastated by the words he spoke. All of my emotions begin to come in like a flood. Tears were streaming down my face, my chest felt like an elephant was crushing every part of me. Everything in me wanted to scream, but nothing would come out. I got myself together because I did not want my children to see me broken and devastated. While sitting on the edge of the bed, I began to block out what he was saying. I started reflecting on all the things that I had settled for to build a life with him. I gave up all of the dreams and desires that I wanted to achieve. Every argument and every beating began to flood my mind. How could this no-good bastard do me like this?

I felt like a fool moving from place to place, only to wind up living with my mother. I spent years of tears and shame covering up his behavior and neglecting who I was. There were years where I didn't share with anyone how it was affecting me emotionally. I went through years of being called a "bitch," dealing with things I knew about the women he was sleeping with, and his manipulation. He controlled my every move, where I went, what time would I be back, what I could and couldn't wear. He picked out my clothes, scarves to wear on my head, even to the shoes I wore at times. Everything had to be in order. I denied the abuse, drugs, and the unstable mindset of a man I thought loved me. Oh yes, he had a way about him that could pull me back in and I would find myself wrapped right back up in the sheets. Yes, the sex was good! But was it enough to stay in that prison of toxic words and actions placed upon me by someone else?

Life has a strange way of presenting itself. It's like getting in a car driving down the road. The road doesn't look familiar, so you turn around and go back. Each time I went back I felt like I was on a roller coaster ride and did not know how to get off. For the next few days, the different encounters I went through kept playing over and over in my head. Prior to this day we had a physical altercation where he hit me so hard, I thought I was sweating from being scared to death. His anger came out of nowhere, but I felt a burning sensation behind my ear. It wasn't sweat; it was blood running down my neck. The two most horrible events that I will never forget was when one of his family members sat in our living room, watched my husband beat me, and did not even try to stop him. The abuse not only affected me, it also affected my children because they had to witness it most of the time. I was not prepared for what I was about to walk into.

One day, I went to visit a friend and because I was not at her house to receive his call, his anger turned towards our youngest son. When I got home, my son had bruises all over his body, a busted lip, and bruises on his face. My oldest son was holding his brother trying to comfort him. I was enraged and all I could think about was killing this man! I knew he kept a gun in the top dresser drawer. Through the anger and tears, I was shaking so bad, I could hardly see how to load the gun. The bullets kept dropping to the floor. Then I heard a voice say, "Is he worth going to jail for and never seeing your children?" I got myself together and left with my children to get to the hospital. Their father (my husband) was arrested later that night for child abuse. We went to family therapy, but when he tried to control that environment, they asked if we could have separate sessions. I hid within myself like a tortoise pulling my head back in the shell when there was danger coming. My shell allowed me to keep the secrets about my life hidden from the world. I was good at keeping secrets and only showing what I wanted the world to see while dying on the inside. I felt like a gift box wrapped so nicely with the big beautiful bow, but the box was empty.

Next came the emotional explosion, everything that I felt on the inside could no longer stay contained. It was not a pretty scene, and I did not care who heard me; I just wanted him out. After he moved out of the house, our third anniversary came, but there was no celebration - only the "What Ifs." What if he wants us to come back? What if I could not resist the sweet words along with the "I am sorry, it will never happen again?" What if I let my guard down? Would this cycle continue to evolve?

Have you ever asked yourself why someone says they love you and you are good to them in every way, then they don't want to be committed to the relationship?

It was a beautiful sunny warm spring day. I was with the boys outside while my husband relaxed upstairs that day. He called for me to come upstairs because he wanted to talk. The look that was on his face told me it was serious. He began by saying, "You know I love you, right?" and I answered, "Yes, I know that." He continued with, "I can't do this anymore." "You can't do what anymore?", I asked. He replied, "Be married." He continued with, "Babe, you are a good wife and mother to my children." As he was speaking, I felt like this was a bunch of bullshit. That was the day I wanted him to feel what I was feeling. I wanted revenge, so here I go, back on that roller coaster ride. This time it was with a man who was married. I became what I despised in my marriage, the side chick, the other woman. I found myself leaving my children with other people to be in the social spotlight. The nights of drinking and sex really amounted to nothing. This married man didn't belong to me; he was someone else's problem. I wasn't committed to him, nor did I have to answer to him; therefore, I was free to do want I wanted. I had my own key to his place and could come and go at my leisure. For the other man, I was no more than just a fantasy that became real in his life. I loved the attention I was getting, but at the same time I was losing my identity because of anger and hate. The deeper I got into the relationship, I began to think, "I'm better than this. I have so much more to offer." That was a turning point in my life. I had to let him know that I couldn't continue down that path, so I gave back the key and started in a new direction. That was my anniversary celebration, a brand-new life. I saw my husband for the last time before I embarked on the journey of a new beginning in North Carolina. It was the day I finally stood up for myself and said, NO MORE!

Even though it was hard and scary, it was a relief to be free from all the pain, lies, betrayal and abuse. I learned from my experiences to never let anyone define who I am, put me in bondage, or take my voice. I rose up out of the shame and guilt of my former life and now I was free to embrace my dreams. You can also be free of the shame of abuse and control. You don't have to be silent anymore. You can let your voice be heard. I did it, so can you. I found love again with a man who is supportive of my dreams and desires. I also returned to my first love, the Word of God. The path I took was amazing -- serving as a Correctional Officer for 18 years before retiring. Serving as a Guardian ad Litem (the voice for abuse and neglected children). Volunteering as an EMT (Emergency

Medical Technician), I joined a Mission Ministry doing what I love . . . giving back to others. I took a healing ministry course, but I didn't stop there. I went back to school and received my associate's degree. There I enrolled in many leadership classes to better prepare myself to serve. I joined a group of women in "Rise up and Rock Your Confidence," which helped me to continue to personally develop. Now, I am pursuing my goal to become the CEO of my own business. There is so much I haven't done yet, but I'm on my way. This is not the end of my STORY... it's just the beginning.

Cleansed and Free, Dear New Me:

I am proud of the woman that you have become. A woman of character, integrity, and compassion. You have become a voice to the voiceless. Your confidence in who you are and what you want to achieve has grown so much. Your love shines through like a beacon that others can see and feel.

JOURNAL

AFFIRMATION

Vulnerable and exposed, nothing left to hide. A voice of strength and wisdom. Never silent again. This is my beginning.

Janet G. Snipe has served alongside her husband Pastor William Snipe as First Lady for many years and they reside in Goose Creek, SC. She's the mother of two wonderful children, Apostle DoQuoi T. Green (Pastor Donna P. Green), and D'Leta K. Snipe-Waring (Dezmond Waring). She's the grandmother of three beautiful grandchildren, London, D'Laysia, and Alathia.

Janet has earned a Bachelor of Science degree in Business Management and a Master's Degree in Health Services Administration. She has retired after serving 30 years at MUSC Hospital. Janet is the Founder of the Fervent Ladies Christian book club ministry and the Co-Author of "Overcoming Adversity: Pushing Past the Pain". Janet has a great love for people and a passion to help others accomplish all God has placed in them. Janet's loving nature, generosity and gift of wisdom has afforded her the distinct privilege to consult many individuals from diverse backgrounds and professions.

Email: j-snipe@hotmail.com

No Ordinary First Lady

Janet G. Snipe

I t was summer break of 1981. I was happy to be home from college to spend time with my family and with my boyfriend of seven years. My boyfriend had received a job offer to work in another state. He told me that he accepted the offer and would be moving. Once he got established, his plan was to send for me. I didn't like the idea of him leaving, but it was a choice that he made. There wasn't anything that I could say or do to change his mind and once he left, we kept in contact as much as we could. One particular day he called on the telephone and told me that he had a dream that I was pregnant. He suggested that I go to the doctor to confirm whether or not his dream was true.

I made a doctor's appointment as he suggested and the day came for me to be seen by my doctor. The doctor asked all of the usual questions, such as when was my last menstrual cycle. I was not sure when that was but then I went to the lab so that they could conduct a pregnancy test. After the test was done I waited in the exam room for what seemed like hours. I was a nervous wreck and finally the doctor came into the room. "Ms. Green", he said, "the test shows positive and you are, in fact, pregnant." My heart started racing with fear and all I could think of was what my mother would say or think. I was so afraid to face my mother with the news, and when I arrived at home I thanked God that she was not home yet. I was so thankful because I had not fully wrapped my mind around the news I received. While I waited for my mother to come home, I called my boyfriend to let him know that the dream that he had was true. He asked me what I was planning to do about it. I thought to myself, "What in the world does he mean, what do I plan on doing? Aren't we in this together?" So, I told him that I was going to keep my baby. Next, I shared the news with one of my sisters and then I called my aunt crying. She said, "Well, there's nothing you can do about it at this point. Your mother will be upset, but she will get over it." I was so afraid to tell my mother because she had sacrificed so much for me to attend college and the fact that I was pregnant would be so disappointing and embarrassing to her.

I did all that I could to hide my pregnancy from my mother. For months she did not know my secret. I wore larger clothing so that she could not see my growing stomach. One day my sister and were in the kitchen and got into an argument. She blurted out, "That's why you are pregnant!" My mother heard the conversation and stormed into the kitchen in a rage asking "Are you pregnant?!" I stared at her with fear, feeling ashamed, and with tears in my eyes, I was totally speechless. Then she said, "So you want to be grown and have unprotected sex when you should have been studying doing your schoolwork? It seems like you need to pack your clothes and find a new place to stay."

Night after night I laid in my bed having a hard time getting to sleep. I felt sad constantly. I was angry, disappointed, and felt unworthy and discouraged. A few months went by and I couldn't take my mother's arguing anymore, so I called my cousin Vera to tell her what was going on. She said she would talk to my mom and that I could stay with her and her husband until things got better at home. I became depressed and wanted to stay locked in the room whenever anyone would visit, but my aunt and cousins made sure I came out. Vera's husband at the time treated me like one of his children and made sure he cooked a hot breakfast every morning for me. There were days that I didn't want to eat and he would knock on the door, and say, "The food is getting cold, and you need to eat so you and the baby can be healthy." I really appreciated them, allowing me to stay in their home, but still, there was no place like home. I missed my mother and siblings.

One day all of my siblings, my mom, and I were sitting on our front porch when one of our aunts who we called "Holy Rollie" drove up. Everyone except my mother got up and ran into the house and out the backdoor to another aunt's house that lived next door. I was unable to run or walk fast enough, so I hid in my mother's bedroom. My aunt spoke to my mother, then came into the house. I heard her ask "Where did all the children go?" She went from the living room to the kitchen, then into my mother's bedroom where I was standing in the corner facing the wall. I was trying to avoid her seeing me, which obviously didn't work. When I turned around her mouth opened up wide in disbelief and she yelled, "Thelma!! Why didn't you tell me this child was pregnant?" Then she proceeded to ask me when the baby was due, who the father was, and if we planned on getting married. The questions went on for at least five minutes non-stop. I just stood there crying and embarrassed. My aunt went into her purse, pulled out a bottle of anointing oil, put it on my forehead and stomach and started praying. After praying for my unborn child and me, she told me not to worry and that everything was going to work out great for both us. She prophesized that I was going to give birth to a baby boy, that he was going to be a man of God, and he would never want for anything. Nothing she said made sense to me at the time, but I sure liked the fact that she said my child would never want for anything.

May came, and I birthed a beautiful son on the 23rd day. Looking into my son's eyes for the first time gave me a strong drive and desire to want more for my child and for me. I knew that I had to do what was best for the both of us. I became a mother and it was time for me to grow up and become a woman. No longer could I feel sorry for myself or let anyone make me feel less of a person. That was it. Enough was enough. I had to say goodbye to the old me. Up to the point of when my child was born, I had spent almost 21 years trying to live up to what my mother and elder family members expected of me. The years of trying to make everyone happy was over. It was time for me to focus on me and my son's future and not what others felt my future should be.

Years later, I was no longer with my son's father and he barely reached out to even check on him. I was at a point in my life where I was just so done with anyone who did not have my son or my best interest in mind. I eventually moved on, and while focusing on our future, I found real love. On August 22, 1987, I walked down the aisle, marrying my best friend. He made me feel important and reassured me that I could be myself. I wouldn't have to worry about living up to other people's expectations because he loved me for being myself. Later down the line, my dearest son accepted his divine calling from God at the age of 17. He is now the Founder and Overseer of Upper Room Kingdom Church and a specialist in spiritual warfare and deliverance. I became a First Lady and accomplished a big goal I had set for years. I was able to go back to school and not only receive my Bachelor's degree but a Master's degree as well. God even gave me the vision to start a Christian book club ministry in which I named "Fervent Ladies," and we are about to expand to other states.

Looking back on my life then, and looking at where I am now, I have a message of victory and triumph. To the women who have had children out of wedlock, don't get or be discouraged. Life does not stop there, as most people will say. I am an example that you can still achieve your goals and become the best you can be. You do not need approval from others, for your approval should come from the Lord Jesus Christ. When we put our trust in Him and not the world, we are no longer doing what the world expects but what God expects.

Sometimes the enemy will throw different trials and tribulations your way to get you off course, but you must remember Genesis 50:20 ERV states, "It is true that you planned to do something bad to me, but really God was planning good things". God's plan was to use me to save the lives of many people, and that is what happened. When you try to make everyone happy, it can eventually make you lose focus on the most important things. Don't allow stumbling blocks to hinder you from what God has for you and don't allow people, whether it's your family or friends to tell you what you should or shouldn't do with your life. They can give you their opinions and express how they feel, but God knows best. You can cast all your cares on the Lord, and he will see you through, never leaving you nor forsaking you.

Cleansed and Free, Dear New Me:

God is pleased with you and he is the only one who you need to please. Continue to seek his plan for your life and keep your focus on the path that he has already chosen for you.

JOURNAL

AFFIRMATION

Standing on the adversity that tried to claim me. Overcoming my desire to please. I came. I cried. I conquered. This is me!

Kocysha LaShaun is a long-time resident

of Central Arkansas where she wrote her first book, *Humbled by His Grace* in 2013. Five years later, she self-published *Out of the Darkness, and into the LIGHT*, as the first of a mini-book series. She is the co-author and coeditor for the anthology titled, *I Am Who God Says I Am: Living My Life on Purpose*, as well as a Personal Development Writer for *Success Profiles Magazine*.

In early 2019, Kocysha completed the Black Belt Speakers Training and became a Certified Life, Success, Empowerment Coach. She has appeared as a guest speaker for several tele-summits, podcasts, and conferences including Inspiring Nations with Sonja Keeve, Audacious Faith Virtual Conference, and the Today I Choose Me Virtual Summit.

As an Author and Coach, Kocysha seeks to help individuals overcome strongholds that prevent them from walking in their purpose.

For more info, please visit kocyshalashaun.com.
@kocyshalashaun- FB

I Do, But Never Again

Koeysha LaShaun

I DO love sex...absolutely! I DO dream of being married again, even after 40 years of age. But God as my witness, Never Again! Never again will I lay with another man and give him the best part of me only to be shut out and disregarded as some side chic or mistress. Never again will I lay with another man who has not first made love to my mind, and my spirit. Never again will I lay with another man, who takes advantage of my weak moments and vulnerability. Never again will I lay with a man who claims to love what I'm about, but their actions speak differently. Never again will I say the words "I Do" from a people-pleasing mentality, or from a place of low self-esteem. Never again will I say "I Do" thinking something about me will change a man into something he's not ready to be. Again, I DO love me some sex. I DO desire to be a wife. In fact, I feel I'm called to be a wife...but NEVER AGAIN!

I know! Never say NEVER. It seems a bit harsh but let me further explain. Have you ever been in a situation where you prayed, "Lord, if you do this, I promise I'll never again"? But as life would have it, we find ourselves in the same situation again and for some people, it seems to get worse and worse. When I finally came to my senses, like the Prodigal Son, when I finally accepted that my Father had something way better for me than the crap I'd been enduring, I made up in my mind and said, "I DO, but Never Again!"

The day I lost my virginity is the day I also lost part of my identity. At the age of 13, I lay in my mama's bed while she was at work. I was the birthday gift for a guy five years older who had no clue it was my first time, although it soon became obvious. He kept it 'innocent' (for lack of a better word) and respectful the times we were together. I wish I could say the same for the next person. Before the end of my eighth-grade year, there came a call and the voice on the other end asked, "When can I have some pussy?" As if! Nonetheless, to Boyfriend #1, I found myself saying yes, again. This time, the simple missionary sex as I knew before turned into some freaky, taboo 'ish' over the next four years. In eighth grade we'd been grabbing at each other's private parts as we passed each other in the hallway. Ninth grade year, we started having phone sex, engaging in oral sex, and 69'ing each other. Boyfriend #1 gave me a taste of something that I would have a hard time letting go, a taste of something that I began using as leverage for companionship.

There were others to follow: a few relationships, some one- night stands, some friends, some even related to each other. I knew what they were saying about me. I knew how they mocked me. I also knew that I'd become the laughingstock in the boy's weight room where my on and off again Boyfriend #2 (later turned husband, now ex-husband) happened to spend his time.

It was all because of 'one night' in the back seat of my mama's red Neon where I gave head to a guy.

As if that humiliation were not enough, Boyfriend #1 and his best friend stopped by one night for a quick visit. I wish I could say it was a random, friendly visit, but they were really there to openly mock me about that 'one night' in the red Neon. As we chatted, they began making back and forth motions with their hands and coughing. At that moment I knew they knew because I'd had a cold on that 'one night'. As we stood there chatting, I said absolutely nothing, like I had no clue what they were insinuating. Yet internally I felt completely betrayed. And what did 'little ol' gullible, naïve me' continue to do? I continued to be friends with them. We'd hug and laugh and chat like there was no history! EVEN AFTER Boyfriend #1 wanted to see how freaky I was by setting me up with the same best friend. 'Best friend' called me one night wanting to come over. Of course, I said yes. Shortly after he arrived, Boyfriend #1 called, and we chatted for a few minutes. I wish I had a better explanation other than 'it just happened', but somehow, I ended up riding the best friend. Stupid, gullible me! What the hell was I thinking? It wasn't as if he really liked me like that! To add injury to insult, not only was he Boyfriend #1s best friend, he was the brother to my first, as well as another guy who frequented my mama's bedroom.

It wasn't so much that I needed sex as much as the attention it warranted. I liked the companionship, the sense of being needed, and a very distorted sense of belonging. I won't even say they didn't care about me. They did, but we all had a very immature, disrespectful, somewhat sickening way of showing it. While I was the good girl in the streets they befriended, it was the freak in the sheets some wanted more of.

As if I hadn't made enough bad decisions throughout high school, Boyfriend #2 ended up catching a 15-year charge for armed robbery around late 1999, early 2000. He reached out while in county jail and our current off relationship became on again, and on May 8, 2001, at the Grimes Unit, I said, "I Do" wearing a floral print dress in the presence of the chaplain, my fiancé's mom and his grandmother. I can remember feeling sick to my stomach when I first arrived at the women's facility before heading to the men's facility. When we arrived, there was an issue with the chaplain. My good ol' handsome fiancé failed to request a chaplain and the one who was present refused to perform the ceremony. So, guess who copped an attitude? He did. While I tried to remain calm and say something sweet, he was anything but. I felt so ashamed, and whatever dignity I was holding on to dropped to the pit of my stomach. I literally wanted to walk out, but I didn't. Ask me why? Why Koko? Because his folks, our two biggest supporters had flown in from St. Louis. (If you're wondering about my folks. Well, they didn't know).

So, in walked this white male chaplain and before he began, he asked my fiancé if he'd gotten rid of his X-rated magazines.

I can't even imagine the look on my face, but I know I was ashamed yet again. Even still, I said "I Do!" As I'd already been doing, over the next few years, I continued the drive from Little Rock to Newport every weekend, rain, sleet, or snow. No matter how many times he ended up in trouble or in 'the hole' (isolation), I remained his ride-or-die chick. Whether it was giving him a hand job, sneaking in small amounts of weed, and even a pair of shoes one time, it didn't matter. I was down. One month he sent me money and I was so geeked until there was a call about some internal investigation. That led to a one-year suspension as opposed to the six-month suspension we thought would come if we ever got caught. Oh, yeah, we had it all figured out, or he did at least. I just naively agreed.

It was during that one year off that something in me changed spiritually. Near the end of that one-year suspension, he was transferred to a maximum security prison facility. I remember telling him in a letter I was not the same, and I did not want to come into this new unit dealing with the same issues. Turns out, I didn't have to worry about that because he was housed in administrative segregation which only allowed visitation behind a glass.

Before my visitations started again, I'd been invited to attend a non-denominational church. It was the second church of its kind that I'd been to, which was totally different from my Baptist upbringing. This second time, however, I was more accepting of the mixed leadership and congregation as well as the praise and worship songs. That one decision to try something different literally opened my eyes to what it meant to have a true relationship with God. I found out what it meant to really serve God and love others as God loves us. I don't put anyone or any organization on a pedestal, but if not for this church, I don't know that I would've ever gained my voice back. They helped me grow in such a way that I was like, "No more!" No one told me to outright divorce my husband, which I greatly appreciated. Instead, they prayed with and for me. One man, a prison chaplain, shared with me that he wanted to tell me differently, but he stayed true to God's word.

As my husband began preparing for parole, one of the biggest issues was where he'd stay. Instead of moving to Little Rock with me where I was established, working, and going to school, he wanted to go back to our hometown, which I refused to do. But noooo, he wanted to complain about the Little Rock system and how it would bring him more trouble.

It was after much discussion over a period of two years, seeking counseling for myself and even having the prison chaplain I spoke of earlier come visit with him that I decided I'd had enough. On June 11, 2005, I found myself writing a three-page letter to his mom explaining my position about no longer going back and forth about where he'd parole. I was tired, I was hurt, and I was angry. I didn't feel he was truly ready to be a husband and suggested if he was to change his mind that he go to a halfway house and take anger management classes. I also suggested that we'd have to do counseling before he could step foot in my house.

I wish I could say I stuck to that plan. Although we were officially divorced as of March 22, 2006, I did allow him to visit. We did have sex and went back to our separate ways until September 2010. Recently reconnected through morning conversations, I invited him to ride with me to St. Louis. It was my first time ever driving so far out of town and I didn't think I could do it alone. Having vowed to never have sex again earlier that year, there I lay with him in the hotel room after spending the day with my sister and her friend. After us feeding one another at dinner and even after getting pissed off because he copped an attitude about something, there I lay. He got his nut. I cleaned up, crawled back into bed with my back to him, disgusted yet again for my wasted time, and went to sleep. That was the last time we had sex...the last time I had sex.

While it has not been an easy journey over the last ten years, it's been well worth the wait to have sex and commit to a relationship headed for marriage. There have been some conversations, a couple of situationships, but nothing fruitful or permanent. While I do indeed love sex, I dare not waste another moment giving myself to someone who will break my heart and leave me stranded. I dare not allow myself to feel that disgust again because I gave my gold for scraps. I dare not give away something so precious that belongs to only One. He will come, and until he does, I will wait.

Cleansed and Free, Dear New Me:

You have been made free! Moving forward, you no longer have to subject yourself to men who choose not to see the God in you and how you've been set apart as a wife to complement one. Moving forward, you no longer have to lay with someone for attention because the right man will see how simply amazing you are, how beautiful you are, and that you're definitely worth the wait. Yes, you do love sex and being a wife... But never again with the wrong person.

JOURNAL

AFFIRMATION

*Moving forward. I will no longer
subject myself to anything less than what
my Heavenly Father desires for.*

Roseheather *"Latrice"* Gatison went through a trying time in life that helped to possess her divine warrior strength. She prides herself on building an extremely solid foundation that has assisted women in developing a sound career, physical, mental, financial, emotional, and spiritual foundation. With a goal of expressing, directing and mentoring others through their trials and tribulations with her God given Prophetic Gift and genuine heart she has chosen to become an author.

A College graduate with an AA Accounting, a holder of Lean Six Sigma Green/Black Belt and has a host of strong certifications. Turning dreams and tragedies into true successful visions. Leaving many lost for words of the miraculous supernatural accomplishments. She has touched Fortune 500's to include being in Upscale Magazine, Podcast, taught courses, assist small businesses, public speaking events, motivational inserts, exceptional conferences such as "Girl Let it Go" and more.

Email: Latriceg_@visionaireacademyllc.com Facebook: Latrice Gatison
Instagram: @billionairemindset_1
www.latrice.net

Unveiling Pandora's Box

Roseheather "Latrice" Gatison

Have you ever thought about being with the same sex? Thinking you are not wanted by the man or woman of your dreams. Having thoughts that if you just try it one time, it will not hurt, nobody will know but you and them. Or maybe you thought, this is how I'm supposed to be. I have learned that we all have flaws hidden in the closet. Some flaws others may glorify, and some may be frowned upon. I know I am not the only one that tampered with Pandora's Box, not knowing if it was temporary or a permanent fix. I thought I was going to test the water and see if it would be good.

One day I was standing in the mirror trying to decide if I should cut my hair or not. Should I add tracks, grab a wig, or just whack it off? It was time for a makeover because I just could not take looking ordinary anymore. I wasn't happy with myself due to rejection after rejection from my then-husband and boyfriend. It was getting late, but I promised my friend I would meet her at this party downtown. Knowing the hell I had been through a few weeks ago, I needed a drink and to hear some good music. It was one of those Beyoncé nights when I wanted to grab a short fitted spandex freak 'em dress showing every inch and curve my Granny blessed me with. Because of my style, I reached for a blazer that matched my dress and ran out the door to meet my friends to dance the night away.

This was something my friends and I did when we were completely done with someone. I had just gotten over the lying cheater and mental abuser. I was separated from my then-husband and was over trying to be kept as someone's secret. Jason's wife had just confronted me because she saw my number in his phone. You know Jason. He acts as if he isn't married and wants to leave his wife just to entertain you. He buys you nice things, pays for your out of town move, gives you money, knowing you will never sleep with him. Yeah!! THAT JASON!!

See, I was over all of that. At the time, things were done for convenience. If I needed cash because my income was extremely low, I would use my seduction tactics to lure him in. As a now single mother, I had to make it all make sense. When it came to conversation and my time, nothing was done without a cost attached to it. There were many nights that I sat looking at the wall, trying to figure out what to do next when it came to bills and feeding my children. I couldn't fathom sleeping with someone for money, especially after just having a basic conversation with men that would wire money within hours. After a bad storm in Atlanta that nearly had Douglasville flooded, including my home, I had to move back to my hometown. In my mind, it was a good decision. The only thing is I had to think of a plan and execute it fast.

I began to tease every man that came my way no matter what he had to offer. I still blame it on my ex-husband, who spoiled me from day one. For a man to get me to budge, he had to be dropping continuous dough or move around without contact. I didn't know that it was a cover-up for how I felt because it all fell in place as I needed it to...until one day I fell in a rut. A very nice looking older, military guy that I was dating went back to his wife. She found receipts of bills being paid and numerous phone call logs. He disappeared into thin air. Being in my feelings with anger and sorrow, I decided to enjoy the night with friends at a small party in the city. I would get dressed, showing my small waistline and heavy bottom. Especially after waist training, popping diet pills, and walking for about 30 minutes 3 times a week. Baby girl was FINE! You couldn't tell me NOTHING! My hair was always laid by one of the best in the city (DONLEE), makeup stayed beat to the gods (Shon Sanks) and lip gloss shinning courtesy of Victoria Secret. This chocolate drop felt like she was God's gift to men. Squeezing into my dress, I burst out Young Jezzy's lyrics, "I AM THE TRAP!" Laughing out loud because there was this deep dark evil feeling that I was going to get into something nobody but God could get me out of that night.

Many knew how professional I was but never how hood I could be. I was twerking and bouncing in the mirror, trying to pump myself up for the night. Dominic was at her dad's, and Kentrail was with his aunt, so I automatically knew it was going to be a long night. I proceeded to take three shots of Patron while talking to my best friend, Tiffany. "GIIIIRL I CAN'T WAIT! I haven't been out in a while, so I had to make sure this peach is going to show right." Tiffany asked, "Wait, where the kids at?" "GONE!!!, I said. "Don't ask me nothing about no kids tonight!" We both busted into a loud, obnoxious laugh. Tiffany cautioned me, "Only you, Jasmine. Please be safe." I grabbed my keys and switched out the door, hopped in the rental with the music loud as I flew down the street and across the railroad tracks to the event hall. Nervous as all get out, I was waiting for my hood friend to pull up.

"Ugh, there she is at the door." "She makes me sick with this!" was the thought running through my head. She was always on time and I was always fashionably late with a loud combination of perfume on. Running her mouth, she forgot to call me as usual. Then she yells out, "Okay, THEN FRIEND!!!! So, you are doing it like that tonight?" I was laughing hard but not missing a beat as I thumped my hips across the street to the door. We walked in, of course, with no cover charge prepared to have a good time. After several drinks and shots courtesy of her "homeboy," I was over it.

I had finally reached my limit. "Oh, no, honey, you got two more." As I shook my head, I tilted it back for her to pour one and downed the other. "Okay, I'm gone!" I made a beeline for the door. "Aye, Ms. Lady" "Don't act like you don't hear me, Jasmine" Deep down inside, I'm asking myself what does he really want? Doesn't he have a girlfriend? When he was single, he didn't come all the way around for me. "What's up?" "Where you headed?" I responded, "Home...where you should be going." He replied, "Nah, I wanted to grab something to eat with you." I told him, "I can't last another minute. I'm going home." "Well, let me meet you there," he said. I just want to get to know you better." I gave in and told him, "I tell you what...if you can keep up with me in traffic, then you can meet me there." I jumped in my rental and took off.

In my head, I was praying I didn't get stopped, but I pushed the gas. I flew through yellow lights and barely yielded at stop signs. I knew I wanted him, but at this point, I didn't want to do anything I was going to regret. See, back then, I healed by having sex. I didn't care who it was as long as I had an attraction, but this time was different. He was nice, and I didn't want to grab sex and go. As I was racing through the lights, I looked up, and he was on my bumper. BUT HOW??? I left before him. He had to turn around. I know I was hauling butt through those lights. Oh well, I thought to myself...he's not getting any. We get to the house, and I let him in. My head was spinning, so I wanted to lay down. He promised not to do anything, so I allowed him to come into my room. One thing led to another, and I was on top of him. I was not thinking about anything but taking advantage of him. HOLD UP, WAIT, WAIT, WAAAAIT, THE RUBBER BROKE...right at the point of no return. "UGH, I'M PREGNANT!" As he laughed, I just laid there with my arms over my head. Because I knew how my body was. Every man that ever touched me that I truly wanted I ended up pregnant by. Some others knew about and some they didn't.

Crawling into my god-sister's bed a few weeks later, I just laid there. "Sis, I need to tell you something." I pulled out a dollar store pregnancy test. "JASMINE...girl, don't play!" I proceeded to tell her what happened while I was in the bathroom using the stick. I was extremely nauseated and couldn't sit up long. Tears began to roll down my face. DAMMIT, I'm pregnant. "Call him. Just tell him. You never know what he may say." "Sis, I don't care what he says. I'm not keeping it."

I finally picked up the phone and called him. "Hello" "Hey. Can you talk or listen?" "Hey babe, what's up?" After a brief silence, I say, "I'm pregnant." There was a long pause. "Okay, give me ten minutes and make sure you answer your phone." He was extremely shocked that I wanted an abortion but very supportive throughout the waiting process and journey. I provided the money and even someone to bring things I needed and clean my home. The night before the procedure, he told me he couldn't make it. He proceeded to tell me that a mutual friend's mom was on her death bed and the mutual friend was in the psych ward because she lost it spazzing on the hospital staff. Since I was in pain and morning sickness was getting the best of me, I took his words. During the procedure, I found out I was pregnant with twins.

Holy crap! What am I going to do now? I'm going straight to hell, but God knows my heart. I called him to update him, but he still didn't show up. He just kept explaining the severity of our mutual friend and that someone needed to be there with her mom. Okay, I got it. He wasn't coming, and this is my decision. So, I began the procedure. The option I chose was a two-day process. So, I went home and called a close friend. "Look, friend, he's not coming. I know. I know. Can you just come down and help me? I'm scared now. They said it's two, not one." As I recall, I remember blowing up his phone and not getting an answer until I said the process was complete via text. He then responded, "Okay, good. Get some rest." That was the end of that fun time. No more late night calls, sitting on the phone, playing in the house, or house visits. It was over just like that. Because he was back in a relationship, we pretended not to see each other when we were out.

My close friends knew what went on, but of course, our girl code would NEVER let it out. One night I wanted to know why. Why did he just disappear and not discuss what happened? I ran into the mutual friend, Sara. Sara was full of fun that night in the club. She didn't look like she was just discharged from the psych ward or that her mom was dying. So, after a few shots, I asked her. Just to clear my mind. This didn't seem right and it was wrecking my brain. Not knowing she was going to ask me, "Jasmine, what the heck are you talking about?" "My momma isn't in no hospital." "Does it look like I been on the tenth floor?"

"I'm about to call him cause he dead wrong." When she called, he busted out laughing and hung up. I tried calling him, and my number was blocked. I was at a loss for words. I began to scroll social media, commenting and liking people's statuses.

"What are you doing up this late?" I received a messenger on social media from a girl I used to go to high school with. I couldn't stand this girl. But I was bored and everyone was asleep. "Nothing. Just bored and a little upset." I've always been an open book. But this story was the only one I could share with someone I thought I could trust. "I hate you had to go through that. You're too nice for that, Jasmine. A grown man should never do anything like that. What was he thinking?" "I don't know. I guess it was just a hit and run to him. I just needed a break. Too much keeps happening too fast and not as planned." "Well, I tell you what. You haven't been out in a while because of your little mishap. How about you hang with me tomorrow night at the club? I see your sisters are going." "Mmmm...Okay, let's do it."

When I say, we had a ball that night. I mean it! Drink after drink, I kept pushing every guy away. As the night ended, she drove me home because once again, I had way too many drinks. After a long conversation, we ended up naked together in bed. I honestly don't remember everything that happened, but I do remember she was my comfort. From that moment on, when you saw me, you saw her. Nobody had known that I had a previous encounter with a VERY close friend a year or so before that. She was going through a situation and I went to comfort her as a friend. She began to tell me how beautiful I was and how she had wanted me for years. Then the unforgettable happened. She indulged in me. It turned her on, but, in my mind, I was just doing what it took to make her happy. Anything to serve her broken heart.

You know the seduction I was using on men? I guess it began to work on women unknowingly. For about a year after that, I dated the woman that drove me home. She became my confidant, helpmate, babysitter, and business partner. She began to touch me in ways at the time I did not think a man could. It was more mental than physical. I needed someone to talk to and pour my soul into. My hopes and dreams needed to be explored. I was at a high peak in life, and I needed someone to pour into who would not discuss it with anybody else. That was until she planned on emptying my bank account and running off with her ex. By God's grace, her ex contacted me and provided all the details which led to her getting put out of my house. After that, we never dealt in that nature again.

The last young lady was a good friend as well. It was a deep dark secret that we both kept for years. Nobody knew about the late night calls, trips, videos, or live sessions. It all ended after she forgot a toy on my bathroom counter. I could not do it anymore. For some reason, I began to be condemned and disgusted. I called my godfather and admitted what I had been doing. I told him I was done. There was a series of events that occurred that I was not proud of. He provided me scriptures as we fasted to release the craving of it. I began to realize I was dealing with a spirit. I was hurting and considered damaged goods. I did not realize that over the years, I hid all my problems behind sexually trying to please others. I was doing things that I knew God would not approve of, knowing that I allowed my past to dictate my current life.

All the hurt, pain, lies, insecurities and misleading others that I entertained was coming to an end. I knew it was a demon I was fighting, and no matter how much I entertained it, I had to release myself. It was no longer beneficial to the path I was seeking. No matter how much I was enduring, I had to release that crutch after weeks of silently fasting and praying. I was reading renouncing prayers and refusing conversation with women, and it was finally over. The next position I was put into as a test, I was able to pass. I faced a bed of temptation with a variety of women. I could not give in, even though it was my plan. No matter how much another woman wanted me, I just released myself from a woman anymore. The condemnation I was feeling took over every urge I thought I had, and I was finally released from the stronghold. This is my story.

Cleansed and Free, Dear New Me:

Knowing how valuable I am to myself has become a priority. I've come to learn that no matter what I endure, my mental strength has to remain solid through every trial. I've NEVER regretted anything from my past no matter how damaging some may think things were or who I've let down. They're merely only lessons that anchored me into evolving into the beautiful soul I am today.

JOURNAL

AFFIRMATION

I decree and declare that I will no longer live within the bondage of other's expectations. Releasing the Hurt. Overcoming the temptation. Full of faith and ever-changing. Beautifully becoming me. Forever Free!

Lynda Barnes, a Kingdom Success Expert,
Business Strategist & Ex-Psychologist has consulted with many on business strategies to start and 10X their influence, income and impact through ministry, business and community programs.

She's also an advocate and survivor of sexual abuse and domestic violence and has counseled many women and children on letting go of fear and inner turmoil so they can maximize their capabilities.

Lynda helps you to shift your mindset, get clear on your calling to serve, and also how to accelerate, create wealth and impact in your ministry and business without making costly mistakes. She educates from a place of personal and educational experiences. She coaches from mistakes and lessons learned while building a consecutive multiple 7-figure earning ministry including a mental health practice, non-profit and for-profit businesses. She's the founder of the #KingdomCEONetwork & Academy, Omega Alpha Nu Ministries, OAN Life Church & Christian Academy, Anthony Barnes Concrete, 1Accord Construction and other businesses and community programs.

Featured on Mindset2Millions, Huffington Post, BlackCEO, & other media outlets

www.drlyndabarnes.com

From Prison to The Palace

Lynda Barnes

t was on a cool early April morning before the crack of dawn, the guard said "Look straight ahead" as I got off the Blue Bird prison bus. I walked shackled at my ankles and wrist down the yellow line of this long narrow walkway that smelled so earthy and looked so gloomy. It was frightening to even think of the scary unknown experience that was about to come. I walked in a single file line into a room of screaming guards telling me to strip naked. I thought to myself how and why I was there. It didn't make any sense to me, but my attorney advised me to sign the deal because if I went to trial, I would get 25 years or more. Even when God told me I wouldn't go to prison, even when others told me to change attorneys, and even when there was no evidence other than my financial fines and obligations, I took the deal!

I did not commit the crime I was accused of. You see, I was actually a very successful psychologist that owned a community mental health center. I also created various ministries, for-profit businesses, non-profit businesses, and community programs to create an impact in my community and abroad. I founded a church that was sustainable from the funds of the other businesses and programs. I helped hundreds of people in any way I could because money was not an issue. Yet, I continued to ask myself why! Well, two of my contracted employees, who later became my friends, committed fraud, but it was my understanding that I was the only one liable, criminally and financially.

I stood there naked among 17 other women plus the guards screaming at me. They were giving instructions about the intake procedures and processes when tears started rolling down my face. All I heard was, "Stand there, sign this, turn this way, get your picture taken!" I thought to myself, "was it really true, was it true what my childhood rapist told me?" When I was 10 years old, I was molested and raped repeatedly for over a year. My abuser told me I would not be successful, I would be a toy for others to play with, I wouldn't be loved by anyone but him. I snapped out of her negative thoughts quickly to call on Jesus. I prayed inwardly, "Lord, please help me, please protect me, please give me peace, please show me your love, mercy and grace in Jesus name, Amen."

I prayed and practiced my faith consistently after being saved years before becoming successful. Before that, I struggled with suicidal thoughts, anxiety, and depression. I even questioned God's love for me. It all stemmed from the trauma of being raped as a child and being in an abusive marriage in my late teens to early young adult years. Even though I tried my hardest to prove my rapist wrong, it was a long, tough road, until I found a relationship with God and counseling. I learned to release my fear and forgive any and everyone who may have hurt me. YES, after letting go of the trauma and forgiving others, I was able to focus on my dreams and aspirations of being a great servant of God. This was the beginning of my uphill journey toward success.

I grew in my relationship with God, so he gave me visions and dreams. One of those visions revealed a plan for every aspect of my life. I quickly took action and started working towards the vision. I prayed about everything, mapped it out, and grew a small counseling practice as a ministry. I accelerated the growth of the organization by acquiring a coach, and learned how to restructure and diversify the organization. It rapidly changed everything, and by the third year, the organization was bringing in millions as a whole. As I began to see success, the enemy was not far behind. While I was growing so fast, I trusted others with positions within the organization. In the meantime, I ignored the fact that God gave me instructions. I was to pray over everyone and wait for His answer before hiring anyone. Now years later, my disobedience would cost me almost everything. After years of being a full-time entrepreneur and ministry leader, making consistent seven figures for years, it all came to a halt. I was such a kind-hearted person that I thought about everyone else's needs and practically neglected my own. When all was said and done, everything in my bank accounts was frozen by the Feds.

I was sentenced to 20 months in prison, but I did 18 months with good behavior. I went to a work release program for the last eight months of my sentence. While in prison, I became engulfed in God's peace. I studied God's word even more, prayed more, fasted more, asked for guidance, and listened to hear HIM more. I became a person everyone would talk to about their issues and problems because I was Dr. Lynda. As the time neared for my release, here comes the enemy with a planned attack. Would it be the end of me, or would it make me stronger? The enemy tried to stop my release, tried to get me sent back to prison from the work release program over a technical issue, tried to stop my family from coming to see me, but I stayed steadfast to my faith in God.

"THANK YOU, GOD!" I yelled, "You've seen me through." Even through all the adversity, storms, and mayhem, God was always with me. I learned to rely on God for everything. Little did I know the real storm had not come yet, as I was leaving the facility, there was a hurricane brewing. I, along with my family, had to drive straight through it. This was a real hurricane, and the drive was about three hours before we would make it home. It was super windy and raining heavily in some areas, other areas we couldn't get through because of flooding. It was a very difficult drive home and I prayed the whole way for protection and guidance. We finally made it safely.

As the weeks went by, I tried to get back into the swing of life without bars and wired electric fences. Life gradually became hard for me. I started to doubt myself and I started to feel worthless and unloved. I tried harder and harder each day to hold on to my faith, but my faith was diminishing. There were so many things that had happened in my family while I was gone. I felt like I was left alone like no one cared. I got worse as I started to withdraw myself as much as possible, even from my parents, husband, and children. It became so hard for me to deal that I often contemplated suicide. After years of not even thinking about doing such a thing, the thoughts were back. It was so bad that I would literally sit on the bathroom floor with a knife in hand, with the racing thoughts of the negative things the enemy would fill my mind with.

It was 11:30 a.m. on a Thursday and everyone was gone to work or school. That day was so dark and gloomy for me, I couldn't take anymore. I didn't want to live anymore. I didn't want to be a burden to anyone. I was gonna end it once and for all. I ignored the still small voice that spoke from within, saying "I love you"! I picked up the knife once again and held it to my wrist to make a quick cut across my veins, but just as I was about to make the incision, the doorbell rang. As I sat on the floor, debating on whether or not I would answer the door with the knife still in my hand, I realized that I had cut myself and didn't even realize I did it. I tried to wipe the tears from my eyes and pull myself together to go answer the door. The person would not leave; they just kept ringing the bell and knocking on the door. I thought to myself, "Why God, why won't you just leave me and let me die?" In spite of all the negativity that was flowing through my mind, I answered the door. It was one of my spiritual mentors coming to check up on me because they hadn't heard from me. By God's grace, she was an angel sent to save me. She prayed with me, cried with me, listened to me, and hugged on me. She also told me her own testimony of losing everything but

124

still trusting in God to restore everything, including her sanity. She departed, leaving me a scripture to meditate on daily. "Philippians 4:13 New King James Version (NKJV) I can do all things through Christ who strengthens me".

As time went on I got better. I was less depressed and I started focusing and obeying God's instructions regarding every area of my life. I began rebuilding my life, ministry, and business as God instructed me to. Even when my husband would ask me to get a job, I knew I had to stay focused and obedient. I now understood fully what it meant to rely on God, and that I could do all things through Christ. You see, I put into practice the same principles I used to overcome the hurt and trauma from my childhood rape and a broken, abusive marriage to becoming a successful multi-millionaire.

1. Correcting my heart posture - I searched my heart to forgive others. Forgiveness brings you peace and prepares you to release and let go of the past hurts.

2. Shifting my mindset - I had to shift my mindset to not focus on the negative things or on my failures. I chose to focus and call those things forth into my life as though they were. I journaled, spoke of my dreams, visions, and desires; I created a vision board and spoke affirmations daily.

3. Initiative and Obedience - I took action steps towards my goals, I prayed about it, asked for guidance, then took action to manifest what I wanted. If God told me to wait, I would wait on God. I decided I would never go ahead of God again.

4. Gratefulness and Gratitude - I was very grateful. I showed my gratitude through my service to others in every way possible, even though my coaching, mentoring, and teaching in various areas of life, ministry, and business.

5. Influence and Impact - I became an influence and impacted the lives of thousands even through my ministry, business, and community programs, and even products and services.

Through my obedience to God, correcting my heart posture, shifting my mindset, taking action, and being obedient, also being grateful and sharing with gratitude, I was rewarded. God restored what may have seemed lost. God restored my family, my marriage, my life, the vision, my success, and I was even restored financially.

No matter what you've been through, no matter your situation or circumstance, hold on to your faith, hold on to God. He will see you through the storms and calm the seas. Never let your past negatively impact your present or your future. Always know that God is with you, and he is available. HIS power is within you so act like you own it. Remember to pray about everything and be obedient when God makes HIS request. Seek help when you're feeling down, surround yourself with uplifting people. Get a counselor, coach, or mentor to hold you accountable and to support you. Don't let other people steal your joy or your confidence. If you don't believe in you, no one else will. Remember, you are loved by God always, and he is everything. God gave his son Jesus to save you. In order to live a fulfilled, successful life, we must operate in our calling. God has given you a call to serve. I now continue to help others start or 10x their ministry, business, and community programs.

Cleansed and Free, Dear New Me:

You should be so proud to release what held you back. With the help of God, you are obedient to your calling. This will transform ministries, businesses, and community programs that create impact and influence in the lives of others. You are building God's kingdom. #kingdomceonetwork

JOURNAL

AFFIRMATION

I can do all things through Christ.
Who gives me strength.

Michele Green is the mother of Bryant McKinnie, Jr. Bryant played in the National Football League for 12 years and winning a Super Bowl with the Baltimore Ravens. Michele is the past President of the Professional Football Players Mothers Association.

Once Bryant completed college and retired from the NFL, Michele resumed her studies in Christian Ministries.

As a member of The Perfecting Church, Michele is an active participate at Hope Mobile, which is a monthly ministry providing food to those in need.

Michele is the recipient of the Presidential Lifetime Achievement Award from President Obama for Community Service. Michele is also an author with her first book named, Entitled. It is about her life as a single mother in the NFL and how easy it is to drift from one mindset to another, to go from humble beginnings to entitlement.

Michele can be contacted at https://www.facebook.com/michele.green.902 and IG: @4shellygirl

Sweet Nothings

Michele Green

hat are soul ties? I never heard of that. Is there such a thing?
Are soul ties ungodly? Well at my age, 64 years young, I found
out what it is and yes, it is real and dangerous. For me, it was
an emotional tie, physical through sex, and a covenant through spirit
with someone who I was intimate with. This person took over my whole
soul, body, and mind for 20 years! The day you become one with another
is when you engage in the physical act of sex. You try to get rid of them,
stop thinking about them and consistently wonder if they going to call
you or stop by. You move away and you find yourself, years later, still
thinking what it was like. You're still dreaming about all the good times.
You still feel like a part of you is with them and they are with you. Soul
ties are a spiritual bond in a relationship, and God is the only one that
can free you when it is not rooted in him. When you're married, a soul tie
is supposed to bring you and your spouse closer together intimately and
in your relationship with the Lord. However, if only one of you is in the
Lord and the other is not, that becomes a problem because you think "I

am saved so I can save him". You don't want to give up and you tell yourself, "I am not going to give up"! This goes on for years! You want to give it up, but you are in too deep! God is not anointing this relationship. This is mess, girl you need to RUN!

I remember clear as day, school was out for the summer and it was 7 a.m. I got a call from my aunt at the last minute to come and babysit her kids. I was mad because I was sleeping and it was my vacation from school. I marched down the steps, said "good morning" as it was a custom to speak when entering a room. My grandfather was eating his breakfast before leaving to go to work at the plant and I breezed by him with a half behind "good morning". I did not realize that this would be the last "goodbye" I would say to him! I was sixteen and babysitting was on my terms and definitely not at 7 o'clock in the morning. I only had to go a couple houses down from my house, but it was the principle of getting up early.

On my way back home from babysitting, I saw so many cars and people at my house in the middle of a weekday! When you see this, you know something is up. You see, I lived with my grandparents during the late sixties in a neighborhood where everyone knew everyone. This was a time when neighbors would holler at you and tell your grandparents what you did. This was also a neighborhood where when something happened the neighbors came running, bringing groceries and anything else they thought you needed. On this particular day, I was devastated to find out my grandfather died. Our house was packed with folks. I was the first grand and I had a close relationship with my grandfather. I was the granddaughter who wanted to please him, especially since I was a girl. I wanted him to be proud of me.

I never grieved for my grandfather, but I later realized that my boyfriend at the time was the person that I used to transfer the feelings that I had for my grandfather to. He became my comforter, my go to, the man in my life. He had me--not sexually, but in my heart and I was in love. We broke up after some months but I decided I was not giving up the goods yet. Eventually, we got back together. Back in the day it was called "messing around", because we did not have the title of boyfriend/girlfriend. One thing led to another and boom the soul ties began. I was so entangled that I was blind to it. Everyone saw it but me. All I knew was that I was madly in love. I was on the phone late at night talking until one of us fell asleep on the other end. Talking about nothing, but I willed all night that that call would not end.

All through high school and college, it was still the same thing. I dated others, but I was his main chick. I was in, hook, line, and sinker. The tie was so strong, there was no coming out, and it did not matter what he did. Forgiveness was always an option. I was mad for a minute, feelings would come into play, and I started missing him no matter how much I tried to stay strong. He would find a way to get in because he knew he had me.

"The one who is the taker is the controller of the relationship. The giver, because of fear or rejection, usually submits and gives of themselves to the other, to keep the peace

while losing themselves in the process. The controller controls the other person to get them to perform to meet their need of love." (1)

This on again off again is like a cycle -- a ferris wheel stuck and will not stop. I want to get off, Lord, help me! I promise I will not do it again! It's okay during the week, because I am busy working and I am distracted, but the weekend comes, and I think I made it, he won't be coming, I am safe. Then, there is a knock at the door or a call on the phone "saying it's me, let me in". What do I do? Let him in!

"God, why can't I stop this cycle?" "I know this is not of you". I felt like I was in a spiritual warfare and I was losing. This went on for years. The main chick, faithful, always there welcoming him with a smile. The lustful desires take over and when I'm horny I can't seem to satisfy that hunger. Our bodies are to be valued; we cannot treat our bodies like we treat our hunger for food.

Fast forward, baby make three! Just because you have a baby with the dude you been with off and on with since high school, does not mean y'all getting married. We good, life is good, but now it's me. I am trying to make up for what I thought I lost. I'm out partying till the wee hours of the night and he is home watching the kid. What is wrong with this picture? What was wrong with the picture was it finally dawned on me that I was not ready to be tied down; after all that, I thought he was the one.

I continued to be involved in the shenanigans, the off and on, plus one. Nothing changed and this goes on for 20 years! It's amazing how when I finally got myself together, I realized that we did not have anything in common. You know the saying, "I know you like the back of my hand". This was true talk, but I really did not know him at all! I knew him sexually, but I did not know his heart. I did not know his soul and he did not know mine either. We really were two ships that passed in the night but had a soul tie that was so deep.

I had a great job, but the commute was an hour one way, so I decided to relocate closer to my job. I joined a gym, made new gym friends and got with a trainer who turned my life completely around. I became more confident, more in charge of myself, mind, body, and soul. As I continued this journey, I was stepping out of self and seeing myself in a different light. I was now on the outside looking in and I did not like what I saw. I started hanging out with my gym friends who kept me positive. My mindset started to change. It is hard to see the mess you are in while you are in it. What was I getting out of that relationship? Was that relationship going to help push me towards God or take me away? After this new journey, weight loss and new friends, I came to the conclusion that the negatives outweighed the positives. I determined that we must continually be renewed in our mind, especially when we are not really going to God, and when we are trying to handle the situation by ourselves. I wanted to help God in this one-sided relationship. I finally had a come to Jesus meeting with myself. Jesus had renewed my mind, body, and soul! I had become a new creature in Christ. I Corinthians 6:12,13 (TPT) says "it's true that our freedom allows us to do anything, but that doesn't mean that everything we do is good for us. I am free to do as I choose, but I choose to never be enslaved to anything. The body was not created for illicit sex, but to serve and worship our Lord Jesus, who can fill the body with himself." God wants us to walk in His Kingdom; he cannot bless something he is not in the middle of. Pray with boldness! David went boldly to God and told Him what was on his mind! God wants us to do the same! Humbly we bow, with a clear heart, we are not supposed to be afraid to talk to God about what we are thinking and feeling. Psalms 6:1, 2, 4(TPT); "No Lord! Do not condemn me. Do not punish me in your fiery anger. Please deal gently with me, Yahweh; show mercy, for I am sick and frail. I am fading away with weakness. Heal me, for I am falling apart. Yahweh, return to me and deliver my life because I know your faithful love is toward me." Thank you, Lord, for your Grace and Mercy. "In every battle, take faith as your wrap around shield, for it is able to extinguish the blazing arrows coming at you from the evil one! (Ephesians 6:16 TPT) Pray passionately in the Spirit. The consequences cause interference in our relationship with God and it allows the door to be opened for the enemy to come in.

Do not think it is over! When the enemy thinks there is leverage, he will try to wiggle in. I remember over the last couple of years, waking out of my sleep, saying, "What in the world? Why was I dreaming about this person? Why, all of a sudden, am I thinking about him? Is it a sign that we need to get back together?" I would think of him when my guard was down and those thoughts kept coming. In my mind I was like, "well, is there something still there?" God shows us our future, but we keep looking at our past! We must move into action! The enemy is very clever when it comes to distracting you from the Lord.

God assumes full responsibility for our needs when we obey Him and honor Him. I can now say that I am an overcomer. The soul tie has been broken. The soul tie kept me in a place of fear, loneliness, and self- doubt. Thank God, I have overcome the battle of fearfulness, loneliness, self- doubt, and insecurities. When these sneak attacks approach, pray! Immediately go into prayer. When the devil tried to tempt Jesus, Jesus fought with the Word and brought His thoughts under authority. You have the power to call out strongholds and be delivered from soul ties in your life.

Words kill, and words give life; they are either poison or fruit – you choose! (Prov.18:21) MSG

At one time or another you may have felt that you were held in a prison--held in bondage. God, through His marvelous grace, can free us! We must walk in the faith that God gave us.

I must admit, I felt embarrassed and ashamed after studying "Soul Ties". I felt like I wasted so much of my time and life. How could I be so foolish to continue in this situation? Looking from the outside, you never know what is going on inside. My friends were like, "You have it all together"! But inside I was a complete mess.

Soul Ties are an emotional connection with someone after being intimate with them, but your Soul Tie should be with Jesus!

Seek a "God" mate, one who will lead, cover you, and pray with you. One who has mental goals and financial goals. Not having a willingness to grow is a sign to not get involved. Your mate should be the one God has planned just for you; you will know it when he comes.

Declare and decree that your affirmations come from Psalm 139:14, "I will praise thee, for I am fearfully and wonderfully made; marvelous are thy works; that my soul knoweth right well."

I can now exhale because I have "No More Residue"!

Cleansed and Free, Dear New Me:

Why!? Why!? What was I thinking? I wasted all those years on one person, but as I now look back, it probably would have been someone else. I had to stop beating myself up for bad choices. I had to stop looking in the rearview mirror and start looking at the full windshield and the road ahead. Thank you, Lord for New Grace, and Mercy. I used to put post-its on my bathroom mirror, words of confirmation and affirmation and speak them out loud whenever I was in the bathroom. Those words helped me overcome doubt, depression, falsehood.

Words like, "Order my steps", "I will continually praise the Lord", "You said You never leave me nor forsake me", "I am worthy", "I am beautiful". Those notes are gone now because I am a strong woman of God who now walks in confidence, purpose and will ask for help adjusting my crown from time to time. It feels good to be Cleansed and Free!

JOURNAL

AFFIRMATION

Shackles removed: ties unbound.
My Soul is free.
My walk with God has revealed the
new and authentic me!

Monique Outerbridge is the Creative

Owner of Velvet Cakes by Gwen. For over 10 years she have been baking specialty desserts for special occasions. The business name represents three generations of bakers: grandmother Velvet, mother Gwen and daughter Monique. The business started from the loss of her mother Gwen to breast cancer. She wanted her mother's legacy to live through her cake recipes. As a result, Molyn mini cupcakes was created from combination of her name Monique and her mother's name Gwendolyn. In 2019 Molyn mini cupcakes won best tasting dessert at the 2019 B.A.K.E Sweet Summer Tastiest treat contest.

In addition to baking, Monique has 20 years' experience as IT project management professional in the financial industry supporting Fortune 500 companies.

With her professional industry experience and creative skills, it has allowed her to follow her passion and purpose with Velvet Cakes by Gwen.

Website: www.velvetcakesbygwen.com
Facebook: facebook.com/velvetcakesbygwen.com
Instagram: instagram.com/velvetcakesbygwen.com

Stuck in The Bottle

Monique Outerbridge

I heard a small voice ask, "Are you sure you want to marry someone with an addiction?" I said, "Yes, I do because I love him unconditionally." I believed our LOVE for each other was enough to keep us together forever. The willingness to marry a man who was an alcoholic and not knowing the impact was a choice I made.

When did I begin to put up blinders and cover everything to hide the shame, guilt, and embarrassment? When did I stop listening to God's voice? My issue was that I wanted to be married and not alone. There was nothing else I wanted to do in life without a life partner. I wanted to build the perfect marriage, travel the world, and build my cake business with a life partner. I felt like Neapolitan gave me that chance. I was the Creative Owner of Velvet Cakes by Gwen. Now I was adding "wife" to my responsibilities.

"Will you marry me?" I was surprised at the proposal but happy I was asked. I said, "Yes!" What I did not realize at this time was what I was saying "yes" to exactly. I had known him for three years and we were now in a long-distance relationship. A part of me was unsure where our relationship was going, but a couple of days before my 40th birthday, I got the proposal. My life was finally coming together and now I had someone I could spend the rest of my life with.

About six months before the wedding, Neapolitan had a medical emergency that required a visit to the ER. What happened that day scared the hell out of me and I believe it turned a switch off inside of me (dimming me light). I watched as Neapolitan was sedated to have his heart restarted. I was scared and was not sure how to handle the situation.

While sitting in the ER waiting room, a stranger walked up to me and said "God said everything is going to be okay and you two are going to make it." I took this message as a sign that it was okay to continue with the wedding and our life would be good together.

What I later learned was this happened before, and it was a result of excessive drinking. Neapolitan had known about this issue and kept it a secret until that day. When we returned home, we talked about his drinking and why he was doing it. He said he could control it, and it would not happen again. I remember him saying, "I don't know what I would do without you. I love you so much, you are my Suga Mama." I looked puzzled after he said, "Suga Mama." He said "I didn't mean it like that, I just meant you are my everything." We made a pact after the ER episode that we would be each other's accountability partner. Our commitment was You and ME and Me and YOU together working to not let it happen again. We agreed to communicate with each other when we faced a challenge. I truly believed we had it figured out. Shortly after the honeymoon, Neapolitan lost his job.

Marrying Neapolitan was for better or for worse. I knew that divorce was not an option. It was "until death do us part "...RIGHT??? Did you notice how I got stuck in the bottle? What I did not realize was we were not on the same page. I recall the times when working on cake orders and when he would enter the kitchen, the whole atmosphere would change.

146

My focus shifted to what he was doing in the kitchen and how it would impact my ability to work on cakes. I didn't understand why him being in the kitchen made me feel violated. Baking was my happy place and gave me so much peace.

I would ask Neapolitan to help with cake tasting and he would be happy to meet that need every time. But when I needed him to help with cake deliveries, it was like asking for something he could not get back. All while he was unemployed with no worry in the world. He had every luxury right at his feet; shelter, food, cable, and a nice vehicle to drive. All I needed was his support with the cake business. He felt other people got more of my attention than he did. I slowly began to take fewer orders and put Velvet Cakes by Gwen on hold to allow my husband to be the shining light.

I began to resent Neapolitan because he was not able to keep a job and support us financially. I wondered what I did to deserve this, and why couldn't he take care of us. Why couldn't he see the burden he was putting on me?

I was paying for everything for the household, including health insurance. He showed no interest in being financially responsible. Whenever I asked or discussed finances with him, it always ended in frustration and a nasty attitude. He made sure he got his liquor whether or not he could afford it or not. If I didn't say anything about finances, he had no obligation to add to the household. If I allowed him to, he would spend every penny in the bank account. It made me very angry that he had no interest in finances or at least making better choices. I felt like Neapolitan was only married to me for the money, and he was willing to ride the wave until it was gone. I was tired of being a nice person. I wanted off of this merry go round ride. HOW DO I GET OFF THIS RIDE and change the course of my life?

One night, I realized I wanted out of the marriage because it was killing the person I once knew. I cried like a child that night, asking God to forgive me for wanting a divorce. I began to feel obligated due to the vows "for better or for worse" of marriage to take care of him. As long as I was comfortable with Neapolitan's constant unemployment and drinking, then life was good from his lens.

I had given up and accepted my co-dependent role and took care of my husband. I became an enabler to the behaviors of a person who was not willing to step into the role of a husband. The marriage was missing a key ingredient - a husband. My husband loved me, but he was not capable of being the husband I needed. He only thought about his needs. He felt entitled to whatever he wanted and no responsibility for taking care of his wife.

I was approaching my 45th birthday and knew I wanted a different life than the prior year. I just didn't know how to make that happen. I began journaling with one simple question: "What is stopping you from unapologetically living your dreams?" My response... You are the strongest person I know. Why are you letting another person hold you back? You are free to be the authentic you because God said so. Being a wife is only a portion of who or what makes up "You."

Pursue your cake business with your full heart, mind, body, and soul. Go after that multi-million-dollar business idea for "good" cake. Keep your recipes original and take no short cuts to make your millions. Don't ever feel guilty about wanting more out of life. Create that new business venture. Start planning the ultimate travel adventure and start putting funds away.

You are deserving of what you desire from your spouse. He should be the provider and support your dreams. Demand him to step up in his role. Stop allowing him to have a pass on not being present for you.

You don't need permission. Your spouse will either be on board or not. Life is meant to be lived, not to be passed by or to

live through others. If he wants nothing out of life, then he has to own that, not you. Be bold and move forward with your life.

During my journaling, we decide to go to counseling and we discussed everything that was going on in the marriage. We discussed the drinking and how it had impacted our relationship. By the third session, Neapolitan booked a plane ticket back to his hometown. He LEFT ME! He said it was too difficult for him. He just left with no concern about how it would impact ME.

Funny thing is I did not realize he left me until I was at the gym working out, replaying the counseling sessions in my mind. I was walking on the treadmill looking out the window, watching the cars pass by and saw a grey pickup truck pass by the window. It reminded me of Neapolitan's truck, and then I stopped mid-stride, paused the treadmill, and my eyes filled with tears. My personal trainer turned to look at me and realized I had an emotional breakdown in front of her. She grabbed me just before I fell apart and held me while I cried. I remember her clearing the room to give me some privacy. The cry I had that day was like someone hit me so hard in the gut I could not breathe. That day the gym became my safe place.

His leaving broke something inside of me, and the pain was deep. I never left him, not once during the entire marriage.

At that moment, I blamed myself for him leaving, but that was far from the truth. These are the thoughts of a person stuck in the bottle of her situation. My reality was I was supporting all of Neapolitan's addictive behaviors. I thought I was the reason for him leaving, that I pushed him away. This was when I realized I needed help...I was a co-dependent for an alcoholic.

Neapolitan came back home after some time and we discussed what was needed for things to work. I decided to give him one last chance to step up in the marriage. Things were great for a while; he was working and not drinking. I felt like we were turning a corner in the marriage...I had HOPE. But soon things changed back to no job and drinking. As a co-dependent, I found myself constantly watching his every move. Meaning, if we went out for social events I made sure he didn't drink too much. I checked the bank account to see where money was going. I started to ignore the drinking patterns because I thought maybe if I did not watch or say something, things would get better. Unfortunately for me, they did not. I also realized I could not fix Neapolitan or the addictive behavior; no amount of love could. My heart was broken. I was scared, ashamed, and just so tired.

A few months before my 45th birthday, I prayed to God to help me because I couldn't carry this burden anymore...I wanted peace and happiness.

By the fall of 2017, my life changed. I was on a girl's trip to Hawaii to celebrate a friend's 40th birthday. I made a commitment to God that I would get up at sunrise every day and spend time with him and journal if the Spirit moved me. Midway thru the trip, I was able to hear God's voice so clearly. I asked, "WHERE AM GOING, and HOW do I proceed with my life?" I heard a voice say, "You are ready to be alone...trust me fully." I thought I was hearing things. I sat there again, began to journal, and heard it again, "You are ready to be alone...trust me." I looked around, but there was no one there but me sitting by the water. CLARITY and a PEACE fell over me, and tears just fell from my eyes. All this time, I didn't think GOD could hear my pleas for help. God heard me thru the prayers, thru the tears, and when I could not speak, God read my heart. God had been listening all the time. He just needed me to let go and stop trying to fix what he was designed to fix.

I left Hawaii and begin implementing the plan that would free me to live God's way. GOD had forgiven me for marrying without his permission. He forgave me for not trusting him. God sent me so many signs, but I was blind and could not see them. This was my lesson to learn. God never left me; I just stopped seeking God for direction on his life plan for me. God's Spirit lives in us, and when we disconnect from it, we are not in alignment with his purpose for us.

Sometimes we have to let go of someone we truly love and let God take over his divine purpose.

I had to work thru the hurt and pain I had self-inflicted because of my desire to control God's life plan. I had to re- build my faith in God and

150

know he is the source of everything. All I needed was some faith the size of a mustard seed and to let God do the rest.

Trusting God, I filed for divorce. I was no longer stuck in the bottle. Breaking free required the glass of self-control, people-pleasing, and fear to be shattered.

Cleansed and Free, Dear New Me:

Today I am healed from a life of co-dependent behavior and fear of not being enough. This divorce was my freedom ticket and there is no more residue. God is my source, and he continues to guide me in all aspects of my life.

I am not perfect, but my life is perfect because God is in control. Divorce is not a death sentence and God does forgive you. Just hand it over to him and let him carry the burden.

God has given me a second chance at life and I am living unapologetically. I have restarted Velvet Cakes by Gwen, and I am not dimming my light anymorc.

JOURNAL

AFFIRMATION

Staying true to myself. I accept who I am. Strong, confident, and beautifully living unapologetically. I am love.

Roz Knighten-Warfield is an Amazon

Best Selling Author and Smileologist! She is CSO (Chief Smile Officer) for Stop It & Smile, ZOR Consulting Group and S.M.I.L.E, Scribe & Write. Roz is an amazon bestselling author of multiple projects, speaker, relational currency strategist, mentor, wordsmith creator, and prayer warrior. She is certified by Coach Academy International. She passionately enjoys collaborative measures and effective partnerships amongst men & women who desire to lead lives full of zeal, clarity and courage.

Roz has been featured on CPW Media, Love & Light with TDR, TBN, Shani and Friends Radio, Venessa Abrams Radio, and hosted many platforms. Roz believes in Living Your Best Life and S.O.A.R (Surrendered, Obedient, Abiding, Radically). Roz resides in Dallas, Tx with your BOO (Beloved Only One), Vincent Warfield, they have 3 children and 2 grandchildren.

Reach out to her at
https://www.facebook.com/rozknightenwarfield
Instagram: @rozknightenwarfield
website: www.rozknightenwarfield.com

The Party That Broke Me

Roz Knighten-Warfield

T he day I realized a bachelorette party would save my life was the day I realized second chances are tangible and that my spiritual DADDY indeed loves me! Are you haunted by emotional triggers that pop up from time to time that make you vomit? Are you mentally stuffing your greatness and brilliance like a trash compactor because of past decisions made? Are you living in the shadows of Ms. Church Girl or Brother Do Right? Are you out of fellowship with God and brawling to be a kingdom disciple? Do you attend church services every Wednesday and Sunday and have become immune to living a double agent life? Well, these are some of the actions and thoughts I performed for years. Reality hit strong, "Roz, do you want to live or die?" Keep in mind that I was not only playing hide and seek with those very questions, but I was also playing hide and seek with God for years.

Quote of Hope by Dr. Tony Evans: God can take the good, the bad, and the ugly and create a masterpiece called your destiny.

Scripture: 2 Corinthians 5:17 Therefore, if anyone is in Christ, he is a new creature; the old has passed away, and see, the new has come! Christian Standard Bible (CSB*).

My hope is, that as I share this story, it will help you to press, push, pray and praize with a "z", your way into new soundness of confidence and assurance to live your best life NOW! The residue of these thoughts and actions caused regret, shame, guilt. This residue also caused fear of what others would think of me if they knew or found out about my dark, cluttered closet of skeletal bones of condemnation, conviction, and lies. Allow me to share a story that not only broke me but saved my life.

When I was in my twenties, I lived a carefree life. I was an excellent employee who traveled and made good money and I enjoyed doing whatever the heck I desired to do. I was dumbfounded when it came to how I should respect self-preservation, self-care, and self-worth of my spirit, mind and body. I straddled the fence and played a back and forth game of tennis by myself, in my own head. I was fighting the monster called "my ego". I was trying to mix the pleasures of the world with faith-like ingredients to make up a tasty cake. I justified my actions by repeatedly telling myself that I deserved this life of leisure because I had been molested by the babysitter's son. I told myself that because of the bullying of so-called friends, the divorce of my parents and all the wrong choices I made, I was too unsalvageable to live a God-styled life.

The activities in my twenties were not the beginning of an on and off love affair with drugs, so let's roam down memory lane and I'll share where it all started. Be advised that the favorable and not so favorables of the party that broke me, but saved my life, will be revealed in a moment. As a kid, the majority of the folks I knew always wanted to be jocks, cheerleaders, cosmetologists or R.O.T.C. cadets in Park Hill, Denver, Colorado. In 1976, while I was in high school, it was time for cheerleader tryouts and I desperately thirsted for that opportunity. When I tried out for the squad, I was told that I was too stout, which was a gracious way of saying that I was too fat. I may have been "too stout," but boy, could I dance! I passed the test and became a squad member, but you know, there is always someone who wants to rain on your parade. The team's captain dogged me out to no end and made me do more workouts than the rest of the squad. She said it was for my own good.

Many were shocked at how well I performed, even though I was not the average black Barbie doll. There was someone within my high school at that time who felt sorry for me and my fat. I was introduced to the in-house drug dealer and was given a pill bottle of white powder called speed. I snorted it or put it under my tongue. It tasted horrible. (Speed [methamphetamine, $C10H15N$] is a potent and addictive central nervous system stimulant, chemically related to amphetamine, but with greater central nervous system side effects. It is a white, odorless, bitter-tasting powder that easily dissolves in water or alcohol.) You see the words potent and addictive? Somehow, I missed that bit of information! I was given a promise that it would help me to lose weight and that there were no other side effects to be concerned about. They promised that it would only produce joy and weight loss.

Well, I believed it because in previous years I had watched and known cheerleaders from all across the metroplex. The ones that were stout, chubby or plump -- well hot diggity dog! -- they were now cheerleaders in new bodies. I was told it was the speed that transformed them. This was my first plight that would support successful weight loss, never mind the possible dangers to my life. The girls looked amazing and pounds lighter! They were still living; they looked healthy and performed a day-to-day lifestyle of making good grades and preparing for college. Keep in mind, good grades were a requisite if you wanted to be a jock, cheerleader, keep cosmetology as an elective and continue being an R.O.T.C. cadet. I banked my decision on these observations. The speed must have also helped with academics. In short, I had put my faith in "world" mode which caused a lot of confusion and decisions which were challenged. That poor little girl did not know any better!

Now let's fast forward to the bachelorette party, that moment during the summer in the mid-80s. I don't remember the exact day, week or year because I had never experienced a high that had me where I had no control of my faculties. Quite frankly, I wanted to forget that week like it was a bad nightmare. I arrived days early to California to visit with friends and family. I was excited for the vacay and ready to deal with the summer days of Venice Beach, roller skating in my daisy dukes, shopping on Rodeo Drive, hiking up Hollywood mountain, and the pleasures of great wine, seafood, and other tasties. Even though everything was kosher, the secret of my speed and coke addiction laced within marijuana rolled joints was not known to the bride, bridal party, or my family.

I loved the palm trees, sunshine, and the freedom in California. It was an awesome place to get high and be to myself. It's a mighty blessing I had no desire to live in Cali because who knows where I'd be today. I'll cut it short to get to the details of the party. I'm finally with the wedding party after enjoying my pre-schedule of delights. I'm now in hospitality mode and ready to help with any last minute to do items for the bride and the wedding.

The excitement and all the different personalities left me jittery and in need of a fix. I would often disappear for a snort -- instead of smoke -- generally because you could smell the smoke. Voila! Then my nerves would be calm once again. I called these nanosecond moments my daily feedings of supplemental nourishment. Yes, do not judge me, that's what I called my special stash. I forgot to add this little tidbit: I was saved many times because airport searches were not at all like they are today. What a pompous attitude I had for thinking I'd not been caught! I was off the chain, self-contained in my own world of what I thought were days of blissfulness! But God!

About the time that I was ready for another fix, I was asked if I cared if others got high. I had already been snorting and I remained to myself until I heard the word cocaine. My ears pointed straight up like a Doberman ready to pounce. I'd never gotten high with anyone who was at the party, but many times in college, I was amongst them. It was still my secret. The delivery man made the delivery, and we were asked to leave the premises until the transaction was completed. When we returned, it was a white winter wonderland on every flat counter of the living room. Well, the male stripper was not coming, and all we had was cocaine powder and rocks, wine, and hard liquor. This was the beginning of the night of events for the bachelorette party that broke me but saved my life!

Snort after snort, smoke after smoke, drink after drink, it was a smorgasbord of supplemental nourishment for hours on end. I remember that everything began to move in slow motion, and we were passing out one after the other. Thank goodness we started early in the afternoon because this would have been a wedding without the bride and her bridal party. We finally came to with dark circles under our eyes, complaining about numb noses and sore throats. This was the crew of bridezilla and her posse. Man, oh man, was makeup going to make us look pretty. As we got dressed, there was silence and despair in the atmosphere. We were still alive. Speechlessly, we tried to help each other camouflage the dark circles. We applied so much makeup that we looked like floozies instead of a wedding party of lovelies. We managed to arrive at the wedding venue on time, but we were sluggish as all get out. I had no voice at all. It was a good thing I was scheduled as a maid of honor and not scheduled to sing a wedding love song!

This moment changed my life for new beginnings. I divorced my supplemental nourishments and began traveling a road of being drug-free. My ego was no longer in control; my born-again self was screaming loud and clear, "Roz, you have been spared, you do want to LIVE!"

Due to the struggle and violations to my spirit, mind, and body, I was saved by a whisper of Psalms 138:7-8. If I walk into the thick of danger, you will preserve my life from the anger of my enemies (myself). You will extend your hand; your right hand will save me. The Lord will fulfill His purpose for me. Lord, your faithful love endures forever, do not abandon the work of your hands.

By the time this book is published, I will have celebrated my 60th birthday. Let me say this: It is never too late to be good in the Lord, and good is still never enough. One of my biggest struggles was covering up the secret that led to compound issues of not loving myself and owning my identity as a child of a King. God spared my life for a reason and He used Coach Crystal Cunningham to be a conduit for me to realize I no longer have to hide behind dark secrets, especially when secrets revealed can save someone else's life.

Quote of hope by Dr. Tony Evans: You will rarely see what God is willing to do in secret until he sees what you are willing to do in public.

Scriptures: Romans 1:16-17 For I am not ashamed of the gospel, because it is the power of God for salvation to everyone who believes, first to the Jew and also to the Greek. For in it the righteousness of God is revealed from faith to faith, just as it is written: The righteous will live by faith.

Three Life Lessons I Learned:

1. Create God-affirmed goals using His word and post creative artwork on every mirror to remind you of your wins in being drug-free. #IamAConqueror

2. Avoid situations and individuals that cause you stress. #IamAnxiousForNothing

3. Peer support and walking with God promotes best practices for your new life. #YouAreNotAlone

Today, I publicly announce by exposing this secret that God is my counselor who walked me through my drug addiction!!!

Cleansed and Free, Dear New Me:

S.O.A.R, that being Surrendered, Obedient, Abiding, Radically! The walk with yourself is a daily process. A desire to live a new life and not allow the past to validate your greatness and brilliance. You were saved to serve and guide others to a newfound freedom in Christ living. It's time to spread your wings like an eagle. It takes time to develop a new mindset.

Just stay in His word, be consistent and intentional. You have ACCESS to Him firsthand! Remove the stones of regret, shame, guilt, and fear and look in the mirror at God's greatest miracle. That would be YOU!

JOURNAL

AFFIRMATION

Removing regret. forgiving myself. I am not alone. Embracing my Truth. free to be me. living for God. consciously!

Sabrina Thomas is an author, parent coach, speaker, columnist, and passionate autism and special education advocate who empowers parents to become their child's best advocate.

Sabrina is a mother of two beautiful sons, one of whom has special needs. She has a drive sparked and fueled by her experience as a mother of a special need's son. She works with the vision of educating, empowering, and supporting special needs families through her advocacy.

Sabrina's innate compassion and enthusiasm combined with her love for her son and appreciation for all people living with special needs are the driving force behind her awareness initiatives.

With over 19 years of experience as an advocate, she has become a strong voice in her field.

Sabrina's mission is to serve as a voice for the specials needs community and ensure families never go at it alone and always feel supported.

Learn more at www.sabrinatspeaks.com

A Sea at The Table

Sabrina Thomas

I was finally at the table – or so I thought. I was soon to learn one of the greatest lessons of personal development – be prepared whenever the opportunity presents itself. Prepared to be the "best version of myself" and not by the measuring stick of others.

It's been said that "Everything in life is easier when you don't concern yourself with what everybody else is doing."

This is where I learned to appreciate all that I brought to the table, including experience, creativity, and a burning desire to help others to come along with me finding their places as well. Being my authentic self – confidently showing up and embracing the gifts, talents, experiences, and skills that I bring to the table – is one of the greatest models we can give to those we love and mentor. Trying to compare myself to or be like someone else is an insult to who God created me to be.

After over 20 years of working full time in the hospitality industry and giving excellent service, I had plenty to offer. I had the burning desire to become an entrepreneur in a space where I had life experience--special needs. I knew I wanted to help the parents and caregivers of children with special needs, using the tools I had gained from my own life experience. I wanted to encourage, empower, and inspire others to be confident, fearless, unashamed, and released from fear to go after their God-given purpose.

What I didn't know was the amount of opposition I was going to face and that I would have to confront one of my greatest enemies.

Comparison kills your confidence, makes you fearful, ashamed, and makes you second-guess every decision you make. It stifles you from seeing the great treasure in what you have experienced, leaving invaluable lessons "on the table." When you compare yourself to others, it makes you a very harsh and unfair critique of yourself and makes you feel out of your league, like you don't belong. This doesn't make the next person better than you, nor does it make you better than others, it just means that everyone has gifts and talents specific to their purpose and assignment. One successful entrepreneur, Wayne Nugent says it this way:

"I don't think I'm better than anyone else, but neither do I think anyone is better than me."

Don't fall into the comparison trap. It kills your joy and steals your sense of worth.

Try shifting your mindset to gratitude. Recognize and be grateful for all that you bring to the table – your experiences, gifts, and willingness to share with the world. This mindset shift into gratitude is necessary if one is going to win the war against the enemy, and thief of joy called comparison.

My story began as I was serving as a volunteer ambassador for a local business owner for an event in my community. I was excited about the prospect of mentorship and maybe even a possible feature on the business owner's platform. She had a few training sessions before this event, and I was excited when the day finally arrived.

Because I planned to host my own live event in the future, the opportunity of being an ambassador gave me firsthand knowledge of all the work that went into organizing an event.

On the day of the event, we set up several hours prior and made sure everything was in place. We were working with excellence in our job as volunteers to ensure success. Everyone had a specific job, and mine was registration.

Guests from all over started coming in, and the meeting space was full. People were enjoying themselves, socializing and enjoying an excellent dinner. The business owner was pleased. I was making a lot of connections with the guests and it appeared as if everything was going as planned. All the volunteers were tired from all the day's work but we were proud of a job well done. Ah, the sweet fruit of success that comes from a team working hard toward a common goal!

The Rest of the Story

Two weeks later, we all met for a follow-up dinner to debrief. I was looking forward to seeing the ladies again. I was feeling good about myself and I looked cute too! My hair was done, I had on a nice pair of jeans, my boots were fierce, and I anticipated a fun ladies' night.

Let me "set the table" for you. I sat confidently with my peers, the room buzzing with excitement as we made small talk and awaited our esteemed hostess.

We (the volunteers) got there before the business owner and we agreed that we were all going to ask to be speakers at her next conference. She had announced at her most recent conference that she was hosting another one the following year. When she finally arrived we ordered our food and drinks. I ordered a delicious Caesar salad with grilled salmon with a cosmopolitan martini! Everything was perfect...up to this point.

The Truth Hurts

As we all shared an update of our lives since the conference, it further set the tone for a relaxed atmosphere in which we felt appreciated and valued.

She (the business owner) shifted the conversation to the conference. She inquired about our availability to serve in the same capacity "as volunteers" for the conference next year. Taken aback, neither of us spoke, so she turned to me, "Sabrina, you go first."

Now, remember we had all talked about this prior to her arrival, so I was ready. I took a deep breath and said, "Yes, I am available and would love to serve at your conference next year, but as a speaker, this time."

Saying nothing, she pulled out her cell phone and went to my social media sites. There was silence in the room as she scrolled. I felt like I was in a hot, boiling fishbowl. She then asked for my Instagram handle. More silence as she continued scrolling...this time, staring into her phone, she looked up at me with what I can only now describe as condescending disbelief.

After what seemed like an eternity, finally, she spoke:

"You have such a low following on your social media sites and I can't have someone like you on my platform with the people I'm trying to attract. Get your following up, update your website, take a few of my courses, and then maybe I will consider having you on my platform."

She then chuckled and started another conversation as though she had just announced the weather.

I was beyond shocked! I felt like I had just been given an uppercut by a vicious opponent!

I was already dealing with a lot of negative emotions like fear, doubt, and rejection before putting myself out there like this. This woman, whom I considered to be successful at what I wanted to do, just cavalierly ripped me to shreds, in public no doubt! I almost felt physical pain.

I immediately became defensive as I thought, "I just volunteered for this woman's event, which took months of preparation. She already knew that I was just starting out. What happened to all the 'sisters gotta look out for each other' talk?"

The other volunteers were speechless. They didn't dare put themselves out there after witnessing my demise.

Suddenly the dinner that had begun on such a nice note left a bitter taste in my mouth. I couldn't wait for it to be over. We said our goodbyes, and that was the last time I saw my "would be" mentor. Now the other volunteers and I still connect, but we never went to another one of her conferences again.

On the way home that day, I called my girlfriend to vent. I was angry and deeply hurt. How dare she embarrass me like that! Who did she even think she was?! Yes, I needed to update my website. Yes, I needed to grow my online community and following. However, as a leader herself and woman in business, she could and should have been a lot more courteous and respectful in voicing her opinion.

My girlfriend asked me:

"What the hell did you say to her?" "Nothing" I responded,

When she asked me why not, I stated that it was because of the crowd in the room, but the truth is – I lacked confidence. She had dismissed me and I let her do it! I was upset with myself, embarrassed, and in disbelief. Disappointment overwhelmed me as I allowed this woman to tell me who I was and what I bring to the table. I didn't even defend myself, nonetheless the other women. I had a voice and didn't use it because I didn't have confidence. I can say that this experience caused me to work on myself and it gave me what I needed to move on.

I believe that when we've been blessed to be on a platform, we have the responsibility to build and pull others up with not only our words but with our actions as well.

All Things Work Together for the Good

God brought good out of that ugly situation though, because that woman's hurtful words served as part of the wakeup call that I needed. Even though I was upset, I went home and decided to make changes.

Yes, I was approaching fifty and had worked the same job for over 20 years. I kept asking myself whether I had what it took to make an impact, because honestly, I felt inadequate compared to the others who were already in the special needs' education space.

The questions came in their full force. Did I know what I was doing? How was I going to finance my business? Did I have enough to offer? I was terrified of leaving the job I had enjoyed doing for so many years. I kept procrastinating but my heart would not let me off the hook. It kept telling me, "Girl, just go for it; you can do it!" Deep down, I knew I would feel as though something was missing if I didn't step out, so I did.

My Next Move

Lesson learned – Be prepared for the next time I'm offered a seat at the table. In fact, I have what it takes to make my own table, I just need to work the presentation. If there's anything I've learned on my life's journey, it's that there will always be fear. Fear of the unknown, fear of failure, fear of rejection, fear of not being good enough, even the fear of success. I realized that nobody else was going to move my life forward for me, so I took a deep breath, squared my shoulders, and made my move. I enrolled in several relevant courses and got certifications.

I went to conferences, joined webinars, and armed myself with all the information that was needed. I connected with some wonderful women who have supported me and we uplift each other. I have grown so much from my interaction with women that didn't even know me and some I still have never personally met.

It didn't make any sense to stay away from the very platform that I needed for visibility or to keep dodging potential clients and hiding away from my audience. No more feeling unworthy and full of doubt. So, what if I didn't have tons of followers? I would keep putting out relevant content that would help whoever came across it. I would keep working part-time and building my legacy.

The day I decided to stop making excuses and being afraid, I gained the clarity that was desperately needed for the journey ahead.

Rejection in some form or manner is inevitable, but I realized that comparing myself to someone else (especially on social media) was one of the worst things I could have done. By simply being my authentic self and following my own journey, I gained my confidence back and realized that people loved my personality. I am finally becoming the kind of entrepreneur that I want to be, one that inspires others, but I had to do some internal work first. I started working from the inside out.

Even though I was struggling and trying to figure things out, God was with me and He was redirecting my steps on the right path.

I am aware that someone who is reading this is facing the same struggles with comparison that I did. Here's my advice to you:

You are unique and your purpose and assignment are just as unique. In other words, do you. While it's important to learn from the experience of others, you have to realize that your journey is going to be yours and yours alone. Do not feel you are a failure or less than because you're not at the level the next person is. Celebrate the successes, learn from the failures, and keep pushing.

You are enough. You are equipped with all you need for the journey, but you won't discover this if you keep looking at someone else. Take the time to discover what has been placed inside of you, you will be amazed!

Rejection is a part of life, not everyone will be receptive to what you have to offer, and it's okay. Don't take it personally; in fact, use it as fuel to propel you forward.

The doors that were slammed shut in my face are nothing compared to the platforms I am privileged to be on today and on the impact I have made. I am living out my purpose and changing the world by being a voice and encouraging other parents and caregivers to be the voice for their special needs children.

I was denied a seat at a table, but I am working to build a whole new table and I hope that my story will inspire you to be authentically, unapologetically you.

Cleansed and Free, Dear New Me:

I am so proud of everything you have achieved. You didn't give up when it got rough. You are tenacious, resilient, and a woman of strength. God is not finished with you so stay prayed up, and stay faithful.

JOURNAL

AFFIRMATION

Building my table with Wisdom and Experience. I feel no shame. I am free to be Confident. and Authentically me.

Tamala Bowen is an inspiring author, speaker and motivator. She is passionate about seeing people thrive over any obstacle. She desires to see individuals live purposefully and succeed in all their endeavors. Tamala brings over seven years of experience in corporate America and 10 years' experience in the healthcare industry. As an author, she strives to write books that are thought-provoking, inspiring, and life-changing.

Tamala is sharing her gained knowledge and experience from both the corporate environment and real-life with everyone who reads her books. For her, the most rewarding part of becoming an author is the opportunity to share her past experiences, including successes and failures with others. Tamala is currently pursuing her degree in Business Administration and Healthcare Management. She is proving that obtaining your dreams is never too late.

Tamala can be contacted at:

www.tamalabowen.com, @accordingtotamala on Instagram and Tamala Bowen on Facebook.

The Coldest Room Ever

Tamala Bowen

Laying on the cold concrete floor, I realized the warm tears covering my face were the only thing I could control. I could rearrange the rusty folding tables or restack the cardboard boxes, but, the truth is, this was their storage room before it became ours. The truth is not always pretty and my truth was as cracked and worn down as the filthy walls in this shelter.

I guess from the outside looking in, my life would have been considered a mess -- a slowly winding spiral to rock bottom. It's the way it felt and even the way it tasted on my hungry nights. I'm here to tell you it wasn't always that way. I had a successful career and 7 years with a Fortune 500 company. I was so blinded by my anger that I couldn't see that I was making the right decision but in the wrong way. It left me and my child homeless.

I ran as fast as I could in the opposite direction when I was passed over for a promotion. I had two promising job offers and I let my 13-year-old daughter decide -- Denver or Seattle? So off we went on a cross country adventure to the Mile-High City. The car was packed to the roof with as much as we could take and still have space for us and Miles Davis, my dog. New life here we come and old life be damned. That was my ego whispering in my ear.

I knew I was moving too fast; I hadn't even taken the time to pray about it. I knew making that type of decision out of anger was stupid. But once again, my ego was doing her own thing. I knew I needed to pray, but I was excited about my new opportunity. My spirit was not sitting well, but I chose to ignore it. We arrived in Denver six weeks before I was to start my new job. I figured that would give us time to find a place and get settled. She would start school and we would have a routine in place before I started work. Little did I know my life was going to be turned upside down.

I found a place and paid the deposit and first month's rent to hold it. I needed to drop off my employee ID and offer letter before I could sign the lease. I explained my start date and would bring the required items after my first day. Little did I know the bottom had fallen out. I arrived to work as cute as I could. My hair was laid and face perfectly beat. I wanted to show these people that they made the best choice and that I was well worth the money I demanded. I went to HR as instructed and was told that there had been a hiring freeze. Sometime between the time I signed the offer letter and my now start date seven weeks later. I would not be able to start for five or six months. I was completely blindsided and deflated. That big head of mine began to calculate all the money I had wasted in the last month. What in the world am I going to do? How am I going to survive for six months? I don't have that much saved. Panic kicked in and I don't even remember what the lady was saying. All I could think was, "How could they not tell me?" I could have waited to move. I quit my job!

I honestly don't remember walking to my car. I just remember sitting in the garage of the building praying. I don't know how long I sat there, but I kept praying and couldn't stop crying. What I got was just what I deserved. I heard a voice in my head as clear as the un-tinted windshield in front of me say, "Why now?" I didn't know how to respond. I knew exactly who it was and why he was asking. I just sat there feeling sorry for myself and cried. With tears burning my eyes, I drove back to our hotel room, numb and confused.

The next day I go in to sign the lease and the second bomb dropped. I couldn't sign the lease. It didn't matter that I paid the non-refundable deposit and first months' rent. I even offered to pay two more months' rent in advance. I had no job, no local rental history and just arrived in the state weeks before. They weren't having any of it and they were keeping my damn deposit. I had just enough to cover a few more weeks in the hotel, my car payment, and food. Plus, my daughter needed school clothes since we left so much behind in storage. Since our three weeks were almost up, I pawned my jewelry to get us another couple of weeks, gas, and food. I begged the hotel manager to please give me a few more days, but no go. We were officially homeless and living in my car.

When I tell you, this is not easy to share, believe me, but I know being ashamed or embarrassed will only stop my growth. I have to own this and be as transparent as I can. It's the only way to free me and hopefully help someone else. I got so low I would call restaurants during the day and tell them they left food out of my order from the night before. It was the only way I could get my daughter dinner after school and she wouldn't know I didn't have the money. That trick would get her a meal that didn't come from the dollar menu a few days a week. She caught on to the fact that I wasn't eating so she could. My excuse was I had already eaten so she wouldn't worry, but the loud roar of my stomach one day told the truth. I tried to cough as loud as I could so she wouldn't notice, but she split her chicken sandwich in half and told me to please eat. Embarrassed, I sat there and cried. How could I let this happen to us? I donated plasma and worked temp assignments with MANPOWER while she was in school. I spent so much time applying for jobs I knew something would be just around the corner.

I had no luck trying to find a shelter for us. It was winter in Denver and I had no idea what to do. We drove to the last shelter I could find and still have gas in the car. As we walked up to the door, I held my daughter's hand. At least 20 men were standing around the door inside and out. Still not wanting to admit that I was in worse shape than them, I asked to speak to someone in charge. I was directed to a lady in an office. She listened to my story and explained that this was a men's shelter. She didn't know of any place for us to go. I broke down that night, I begged her to help us. She made call after call, but there was nothing available. Seeing the dread in my face, she made me an offer. She would have a couple of guys move some stuff from a storage closet and let us sleep in there for a few weeks. It was the best thing I had heard in such a long time I jumped at the offer. Some of the men who had beds gave us their mattress pads to sleep on, so we would not be directly on the concrete. The night manager moved his desk in front of the door to keep us safe and we buckled down that first night. I apologized to my daughter and gave her the extra blanket. I wrapped my dog's crate in my fur coat to keep him warm, and I laid there, counting the cracks in the concrete until I cried myself to sleep. I felt like I was the worst mother alive and so guilty for allowing this to happen.

Every morning we got up at 5 a.m. to shower and get ready before the guys got up. The room for the walk-in showers had no door. One of the men would stand outside to make sure no one came in while we were inside. He became our door of safety each morning, and I was grateful. I would drop my daughter off at school and go park cars at the airport until noon. Then I would make sure I was at my coffee house job by 1:00. I arranged my schedule to take my break in time to grab her from school and she would sit in the coffee shop and do her homework until I got off at 6. Humility was still not there; my ego was holding strong. I kept thinking as soon as I get a real interview, I will get us back to normal. I kept praying, but I wasn't honest with myself or God. It took me getting the flu and not having money for medicine or to see a doctor. I gave up, I began to pray and meant it. I listened and as clear as before I heard "All I ever wanted was for you to trust me." I knew at that moment I could not do this on my own. I needed the grace of God to get us through, and I surrendered.

The three weeks went by in no time, but I still felt like a horrible mother. I would watch her sleep for hours and write poetry to keep my mind from worrying. I was still crying myself to sleep most nights while watching the spiders crawl behind the boxes across the room. Other nights I'd lay on that flimsy plastic mattress and count the cracks in the walls. But I was able to see that my daughter was making a big difference in the lives of some of the shelter residents. God was working through her and it seemed so effortless. One of the guys was a recovering addict. He had lost his license to teach because of his drug abuse but he loved helping her with math homework.

Mr. Math Teacher excitedly told us to get ready one Saturday morning. He had a big surprise for us. We took the RTD train across town on a ride that took forever. After walking through a neighborhood we arrived at a bright pink house that served meals to the homeless. There were so many people there, I couldn't believe how many homeless people there were in the city. He was so happy to be able to take us somewhere and do something nice for us. It was actual food! My daughter was so amazed to get a fresh breakfast with real fresh fruit and not canned everything. She said the strawberries and his excitement are what she remembers most.

A guy I don't recall ever seeing before came to me one night. He was very rough around the edges and kind of startled me, to be honest. He said, "Excuse me Ms. Tam, is it okay if I give something to your daughter?" I said sure and stepped close enough to her to see what he had. He told her he worked at the work today/pay today place to get his bus pass for the month. He only had a few dollars left after paying his cell bill but he bought a box of girl scout cookies and wanted to give her half because she did so well on her math test.

Once again, I was broken and in tears. These men who were struggling with their own issues wanted to make sure we were alright. She would help cook dinner after doing her homework because they didn't really know how

187

to cook. I would hear her say things like, "My mom taught me how to make it, and now I can teach you." She was so proud of herself when she helped this guy from Alaska make fish soup. He told her his grandmother used to make it, but he didn't know what seasoning to use. She asked him if he had looked it up online. The look on his face was clear; he didn't know how. She Googled it and helped him get it right. He was so grateful, he whispered something to her privately. I didn't realize until a couple of days later that she was teaching him to read. She spoke Spanish with one of the Puerto Rican guys who struggled with his English.

She asked me if he scratched all the time because he had a drug problem. Sadly, I explained it to her, and she was even nicer to him. Every day she gave me another reason to be proud of her, proud to be her mother. I thanked God for her every day. She gave me the reason I needed to keep going.

Our last night in the storage room, I apologized to her again. I promised I would never let my pride and ego put us in a position where I couldn't care for her as I should. With tears in my eyes, I begged her to forgive me. She smiled at me and said, "It's okay mom, this has been the best adventure." I learned a lot about myself while in that cold and decaying room. Being down does not make you less than. It could only break me if I allowed it to happen. As she and Miles Davis slept, I sat with my back against the wall. In the dull lighting, I read some of the poems I'd written in that room. This one below helped me see that dread and fear are as passing as time. I knew at that moment we would be just fine.

Music of My Soul

The music of my soul could be defined as great jazz
Some days I feel like Billie Holiday
Singing "Sunday Kind of Love" or "Strange Fruit" on a bad day
But today I'm in a different mood
I'm full of darkness and uncertainty
Love and sometimes loss
It's like Miles Davis on the Kind of Blue album
As he plays his trumpet for me, the uncertainty becomes certain
I'm finding my way out of the darkness and into the light
And the smooth, carefree sounds of Boney James enters my mind
And once again I feel free

Cleansed and Free, Dear New Me:

Today you stand strong, humbled by life and poor decisions, but the grace of God has been bestowed upon you. The blinders of fear and shame needed to be removed. They were keeping you from seeing the vision clearly. The plan set in place for you required the new lens of God. Maintain your faith, your strength, and your dedication to your purpose. You are free!

JOURNAL

AFFIRMATION

Mahogany skin, plentiful thighs, beautiful brown, and seductive eyes. Embracing my Beauty. I am worthy and I am Enough!

Veronda Bellamy is an inspirational speaker who provides personal and business development for those with mental blocks. She is also a Nationally Certified Counselor versed at treating all mental and addictive behaviors. Veronda Bellamy is the Founder and Executive Director of Bridging the Gap of America, Inc., an internationally accredited agency, by The Joint Commission.

Bridging the Gap of America, Inc. (501C3) provides outpatient mental and substance use treatment for all ages. Veronda Bellamy is also the creator of the new movement, The Relevancy Factor ® which is all under the parent company, Veronda Bellamy Ministries.

Veronda can be contacted at

www.verondabellamy.com; Social Media handle @VerondaBellamy; or e-mail hello@verondabellamy.com

The Fall

Veronda Bellamy

t was the year 2010. It was a warm Saturday evening. Hubby and I were heading out to see one of my favorite artists perform – Erykah Badu. I was eager to see her perform. Heck, I love to see anyone perform – I am a concert buff. I get dressed up in a black dress and heels. My makeup was freshly done, hair highlighted with blonde highlights, and blown out. You know, the literally blonde kind – not gold – but blonde. It was full of body and volume. I was fresh, I was sexy, and I knew it.

"Whew Honey, let me get these heels on." I ran back upstairs to get my heels. I hadn't worn those heels in a while. They were black stiletto sandals. I stopped to think for a split second, "I know I will not be able to dance long in these. They won't survive the evening." I quickly shake that thought as I bend to buckle up my sandals. This was a special night. A night to remember. My hubby and I were recently married – January 2010. Our marriage had been through some ups and downs. We were challenged with seeing eye to eye on everything. However, we were committed to our marriage and working through our challenges.

Let's back up to Monday, January 25, 2010, when we called our Pastor. He had instructed us to call him once we had our marriage license. Well, we had it. "Hello Pastor, this is Nick Bellamy. Veronda and I have our marriage license ready."

Pastor replied, "Oh yeah, you do?" "Can you meet me at 12 in my office?" Frantic, Nick responded, "Yes, we can." We hurried to get dressed, so I put on some black slacks, a black vest, and a Carolina blue button-up blouse. I almost looked like a stewardess. We jumped in our silver Durango and headed over to our church. On the way, we smoked a cigarette. We were ready but both nervous. Our home was ten minutes from the church. We thought that was enough time for the cigarette smell to leave our clothes. We finally arrived at the church parking lot. "Whew, babe, are you ready?"

"Do you think Pastor can smell our Newport?" "I can't smell it, so he probably can't either," I told Nick.

We pulled up and parked. We got out and walked up to the intercom to be allowed into the sanctuary. We were greeted and allowed in. At this point, my heart is beating fast as we walked towards the Pastor's office. The blue carpet leading down the hallway was like walking on clouds. I remember thinking, "I can't believe this is becoming official." We entered his office and were addressed by his secretary. She welcomed us in and we walked into the Pastor's office. There awaited two witnesses, one being the secretary and the other was the Assistant Pastor. Pastor smiled and asked again, "Are you ready?" We both said "Yes" simultaneously. We were in fear but eager to become one officially. We didn't call any family members or anyone else. The Pastor approached us, and we commenced our vows. The next thing I remember is "The three-strand cord message symbolic of keeping God as the center of our marriage. Then it was time for "You may kiss your bride." Wow, where did the time go? We kissed and thanked everyone that was there to witness our ceremony. We left Pastor's office and walked the long blue carpeted path back to our vehicle. After that, we decide to go and celebrate over lunch. We both could not believe it was real. However, it was real. We were officially one – man and wife. I felt relieved that there was no more sinning. That night we consummated our marriage. Life could never get any better than this moment. I had waited 30 years for this one day and here it is with the man that checked off most of the items on my list. You know the list us ladies make of our "dream man" - that list. Life was grand. We would drink most Friday nights to kick off our weekends. A bottle of crown royal, ginger ale, two packs of cigarettes, and we were good to go. A few months passed by.

Here we are on Erykah Badu's concert night. I was sexy as all get out. A tall 5'9 caramel complexion woman, hazel (amber colored) eyes, long legs, and a silky-smooth complexion. "Yes, babe, this is going to be a great night." I hadn't seen Erykah Badu perform since the performance with her and Jill Scott, which was the concert that turned me into a real concert fan of both of them, especially Erykah Badu. We pulled into the parking deck, driving a white 2009 Mercedes SUV. My husband was wearing jeans, a button-down shirt pressed with creases and cognac-colored dress shoes. We walked into the venue, my arm encircling my husband's arm. I had a brown Brahmin clutch, and wouldn't you know, my feet had already begun to hurt. My husband looked at me and asked me, "Is there anything you want?" I said, "Yes, Crown and Coke."

We got to our seats; then, he walked back out and returned with two Crown and Cokes for me. The first act comes to the stage. At this point, I am feeling very relaxed in my environment. I am starting to stand up and dance with the performers. I was screaming from the top of lungs – Yessssss! I know every lyric to this song. My husband had about two more drinks. Then comes Erykah Badu. The woman of the hour. I rushed up to the stage. My husband politely brings me two more drinks. I was screaming even when the crowd had gone silent.

I kept the crowd going (in my head). The best feeling was singing to each lyric. Then, the song "Bag Lady" comes on and I started to yell. The beat dropped and I felt myself falling. It was in 3D motion. I looked up and my husband reached out to pick me up. I immediately became upset with him. "Why did you let me fall?" "You saw me falling but you let me hit the ground in front of everyone." I gathered my things and stormed out of the concert. I had taken my heels off by this point. I walked nearly six blocks back to my SUV, fussing at my husband the entire way. I was thoroughly intoxicated. I felt myself slip as I was fussing, and my husband grabbed me. He says, "Veronda, I did not see you falling." "I was into the concert just like you." "When I noticed it, you were already almost on the ground." I yelled back, "Shut up, you are lying, you saw me falling!" "You are supposed to protect me and make sure I am okay!" "You failed at your job as my husband miserably!" "I want a divorce and find a way home tonight because you will not be riding with me!" I then proceed to jump in my car. He tried to stop me. "Veronda, you are going to die tonight if you drive off!" "You are too drunk to drive!" "Fuck you," I yelled back and I punched him in the mouth. My husband stopped, backed up, and let me drive off. I vaguely recall driving off and tearing off the passenger side window. I got down to two levels before the end of the parking garage, and something inside said: "Go get your husband." I turned around and drove back, somehow managing to make it right back to my parking space, and he was standing there. I jumped out and told him to get in. He jumped in the driver seat and I got in on the passenger side. We exited the parking deck. According to my Husband, I talked trash all the way home. We were destined for a divorce after this event.

We finally made it home and I ran upstairs to our closet. I locked myself in and called my best friend. At this point, I was suicidal. "Hey, girl." "Sometimes, I don't feel like I can keep going." "I don't feel worthy of life." Somehow this friend knew exactly where I was coming from. She could tell I was intoxicated. We chatted about life. I told her about the concert and what happened. She assured me that my husband loved me and that my life is worth living. She assured me that I would be okay, and I finally agreed. I thanked her and called my mom.

"Hey Momma," I said as I choked back tears. "I am thinking of suicide." I am in tears at this point. "Rhonda, where is your husband?" she asked. "I don't know, I am in the closet." "I locked myself in here." Mom responds, "Tell me what happened." I gave her all the details. Mom asked, "Have you been drinking?" "Yes, Mom," I confessed. "Please go get your husband, I need to speak with him." I ran downstairs and gave my husband the phone. I noticed he was making a bed on the sofa in the living room. "Here, it's Mom," I told him. "Hello," he answered. My mom proceeded to ask him what happened and he told her. She told my husband that she would be at our home in the morning. Mom lived three hours away. I somehow managed to get in bed and pass out.

"Rhonda, Rhonda, are you okay?" "I told you I would be here in the morning." "It's your sister and me." "We are here to help you." "I have found a place for you to go." They are waiting for you. Are you willing to go?" At this point, I was discombobulated. My eyes were nearly swollen shut from crying. My mom took a cold rag and placed it to my eyes. She hugged me and told me everything was going to be okay. She said that I would be safe and that she felt it best for me to get more help for my safety. She further told me, "It's your choice.

If you choose not, someone will be here to help us get you there involuntarily." I was shocked and in disbelief by everything that happened, from what I could recall. I ultimately agreed to go into treatment.

I looked at my husband and asked him, "What is wrong with your lip?" He proceeded to tell me, "You hit me." I felt this deep shame, gloom, and sadness. I would never do a thing like that to my husband. I looked at him in tears and I apologized. "Babe, you need help." I agree. He helped me pack some things and we left. I was admitted.

I walked down a cold and empty hallway. "Please take off your shoes and your clothes." "Please put on these items sent by your husband as they do not have any strings." "He also sent you some slippers." I felt like I was in prison. I looked around and thought to myself, "These people are surely crazy." "I am nothing like them." One of the staff came out and said,

"Mrs. Bellamy, please come to the desk to take your medication." At this point, I thought to myself, "What medication are they referring to, I don't take any medication?" "This medication will help with your alcohol withdrawals and this medication will keep you calm." I proceeded to take the medication.

"Lift up your tongue." "Thank you. You're are all set; you may go back to your room." I asked, "Can I call my husband?" "For what?" "I need to let him know that I am okay because he is concerned." "I will give you five minutes to call him and tell him you are okay. Here are your visitation hours." I dialed the number, and he picked up. "Hi Husband, I wanted to call you and tell you that I am okay. I don't like it here." I broke down crying. He offered me some comfort. "It's okay babe, this was best." "They said you can come to see me tomorrow between 35, that you have to check-in downstairs." He assured me, "I will be there." I replied, "Okay, I have to go. I love you." He replied, "I love you too."

I spent three days in the hospital and then I was discharged. They told me, "We don't know why you are here." I was referred to someone for therapy and began treatment immediately. My husband and I decreased drinking significantly. As a matter of fact, I did not drink anything for over a year. I apologized to him so many times – in fact – when discussion of the situation arises now – I apologize again. He is such a great husband. I have never been in a situation like that since all of this happened. Our marriage is doing very well; in fact, it has never been better. We now have a 4-month-old baby girl that is the highlight of our marriage. We are so grateful for her. I am a sought-after therapist and own a thriving addiction agency. The irony of it all.

Cleansed and Free, Dear New Me:

I am free to live without the need of overindulgence of anything. I am free and content to live within my means. I am free to serve from a place of contentment. I am free because God has given me the liberty to be free. I am free because being in bondage is not my blood right. I am free because God is within me.

JOURNAL

AFFIRMATION

I am free from bondage. I am free from the need of overindulgence of anything. My desires and life are aligned with success and flow with ease.